Timber Constructions

in Existing Contexts

Stefan Krötsch
Manfred Stieglmeier
Thomas Engel

DETAIL Practice

Imprint

Authors

Stefan Krötsch
Manfred Stieglmeier
Thomas Engel

Further texts:
Annette Hafner, Thomas Stark

Scientific assistance: Kevin Späth

Drawings:
Benedikt Glas, Kevin Späth (theory chapters)

Publisher

Editorial services:
Katja Pfeiffer (project management);
Cosima Frohnmaier (layout and editing examples),
Jana Rackwitz (layout and editing theory chapters)

Laura Traub (editorial assistance);
Sandra Leitte (proofreading German edition)

Cover design based on a concept by:
Kai Meyer

Drawings:
Marion Griese (examples)

Translation into English:
Raymond Peat, Aberdeen (GB)

Copy editing (English edition):
Stefan Widdess, Berlin (DE)

Proofreading (English edition):
Meriel Clemett, Bromborough (GB)

Production and DTP:
Simone Soesters

Reproduction:
ludwig:media, Zell am See (AT)

Printing and binding:
Beltz Grafische Betriebe, Bad Langensalza (DE)

Paper:
Peydur lissé (cover), Magno Volume (content)

Publisher:
DETAIL Architecture GmbH
Messerschmittstr. 4, 80992 Munich (DE)
detail.de
books@detail.de

© 2025, first edition

ISBN 978-3-95553-658-9 (Print)
ISBN 978-3-95553-659-6 (E-Book)

Bibliographic information published by the German National Library. The German National Library lists this publication in the German National Bibliography (Deutsche Nationalbibliographie); detailed bibliographic data is available online at
http://dnb.d-nb.de.

This textbook uses terms applicable at the time of writing and is based on the current state of the art, to the best of the authors' and editors' knowledge and belief. [All drawings in this book were made specifically by the publisher.] No legal claims can be derived from the contents of this book.

Cover photo: Joël Tettamanti

Contents

Foreword

Building today needs to satisfy a wide range of requirements relating to matters such as climate protection, resource conservation and energy efficiency. They must all be considered in the planning and design process. Climate protection goals cannot be achieved by climate-compatible and resource-conserving new buildings alone because about 80 % of the existing stock will still be standing in 2050 [1]. The development of existing structures is one of the greatest levers in achieving climate protection goals in the construction sector. Buildings from the 1950s to 1980s in particular have great potential for renovation and adding extra storeys because these structures make up around 38 % of existing housing stock in Germany [2].

Adding storeys by creating roof extensions reduces further land coverage and mitigates the demand for urban housing. Environmental and to some extent economic advantages can often arise from urban densification measures. Prolonging the use of existing structures by renovation or modernization and densification is therefore a worthwhile resource-conserving approach. It creates urgently required residential space, even in already densely developed areas, and avoids additional emissions in the future.

Timber construction is particularly important to the future success of renovating and adding storeys to buildings because the advantages of timber construction can be realized extremely well in this field.

The low weight of timber construction allows the load-bearing capacity reserves of existing buildings to be utilized in renovations, conversions, extensions and by adding extra storeys to existing stock. Although great attention must be given to detailed planning, the high degree of prefabrication results in short on-site construction times. Timber construction has also increasingly established itself in recent years as a way of implementing climate protection measures for buildings. The great potential of timber construction is evident in the combined effects of using these structures as a long-term carbon store, a means of fulfilling current building needs and as an opportunity to create attractive architecture through high-quality construction.

This book provides an excellent overview of this approach and presents a selection of detailed examples of its implementation. It can therefore provide the principles for a wide range of building designs and become a source of inspiration for activating the great potential of timber construction.

Annette Hafner

January 2024

Notes
[1] Hafner, Annette et al.: Holz in der Aufstockung – Bewertung und Umsetzung von Holz in Aufstockungsmaßnahmen. Concluding report on the research project: 2220HV004A/B. BMEL/FNR. Bochum / Berlin / Gülzow 2024
[2] ibid.

Element A Architekten

The Social Challenges of Building

Stefan Krötsch

Europe is living beyond its means. This shows not only through the geopolitical dependence on energy and raw materials but also through the recurring failure to meet our own climate goals, made legally binding by international treaty, and the dramatic loss of biodiversity on our continent. With respect to Germany's climate goals, the Federal Constitutional Court (BVerfG) decided in its judgement of 24 March 2021 that it is not admissible to shift the "high emission reduction burdens irreversibly into the periods after 2030", since "the fundamental rights of those complainants who are still very young [...] are violated by the challenged provisions". "Practically every freedom is potentially affected by these future obligations to reduce emissions, because almost all areas of human life are linked with the emission of greenhouse gases and therefore are threatened by drastic restrictions after 2030." [1] Rather than placing the burden of preserving the planet's habitability exclusively on the coming generations and other regions of the world, it must be addressed immediately.

Buildings, through the manufacture of construction materials, their erection, operation and demolition, are responsible for about 40% of greenhouse gases [2], 46% of all material extracted from the ground [3] and 54% of waste [4] in Germany. Space heating and hot water in buildings make up 37% of the final energy demand [5]. More or less the same figures can also be applied across Europe. The building sector is crucially important to achieving Europe's nationally and internationally binding climate goals. It also plays a key role in all the other ecological problems our societies face and in the necessary adjustments to be made in the face of the already inevitable changes to our climate, because no other sector of the economy involves

similarly large flows of material and energy.

The operation of new buildings has become increasingly efficient in the last decades. In the future, their energy needs will be covered as far as possible by renewable energy sources. For eco-friendly and climate-proof new buildings, the focus of attention will not be limited to the consideration of the time, effort, resources, and money spent on the erection and maintenance of buildings, but extend to the end-of-service life and the termination of the life cycle. Even in Germany, the increasingly noticeable scarcity of resources and the continually growing quantities of waste materials make it necessary to fundamentally overhaul many familiar processes and convert our entire economy into a circular system of material flows. Retaining and prolonging the use of existing buildings is a decisive strategy, because nothing is more obvious than to use what already exists, so that no resources are destroyed during demolition or become necessary for new construction. However, in order to continue to use existing buildings according to current requirements, in most cases they must be retrofit to match technical standards relating to fire safety and sound insulation, barrier-free access and, last but not least, energy consumption. If the efficiency with respect to operating energy cannot be substantially raised, then often the ecological argument for retaining existing buildings fails. The initial advantage of reduced resource consumption would be soon wiped out by the high operating energy demand. Ideally, the energy demand of a modernized old building should equate to that of new construction (Fig. 1, p. 8).

Biogenic building materials have unique properties compared with their mineral, fossil or metallic counterparts: they come from renewable sources, require

hardly any energy for their manufacture and very little for transport. These materials also store CO_2, which actively relieves stress to the planet's climate system, and they present no problem when their service life is over, as they can be reused or provide a source of energy. Building with timber or other biogenic materials has long since been regarded from an ecological point of view as the optimum solution in the case of new buildings.

A combination of the two strategies – improving and extending existing buildings and the extensive use of timber and other biogenic materials – offers great potential.

Importance of building in existing stock

New buildings comprise a relatively small share of Germany's stock. Thus, they fail to exercise a significant effect on the overall life cycle assessment in the context of the ecological transformation of the construction sector. In addition, new buildings are often erected on land where old edifices have been demolished (Fig. 3, p. 9).

Against the background of the dramatic loss of biodiversity that has been occurring in Germany for some decades now, the question is whether still more land can be designated for new buildings, thus leading to increased coverage. As a consequence, all construction will have to be limited to the present urban settlement areas, which will make better use of the existing infrastructure and allow densification (see "The Potential of Vertical Extensions – Building Without Consuming Land", p. 49ff).

In his 2015 polemic "Verbietet das Bauen!" (Ban Building!), economist Daniel Fuhrhop argues that new construction would no longer be needed if the potential of the

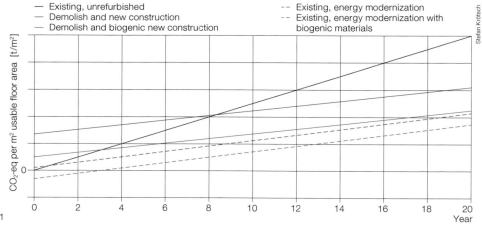

Legend:
— Existing, unrefurbished
— Demolish and new construction
— Demolish and biogenic new construction
-- Existing, energy modernization
-- Existing, energy modernization with biogenic materials

y-axis: CO_2-eq per m² usable floor area [t/m²]

x-axis: Year (0, 2, 4, 6, 8, 10, 12, 14, 16, 18, 20)

1 Comparison of the CO_2 emissions for the erection and operation of existing and new buildings. Although new buildings (red) are clearly responsible for high emissions originating from their erection at the beginning of the life cycle analysis, this disadvantage compared to old buildings (black) is compensated for by reduced emissions during operation, usually within the first ten years. New buildings made from biogenic building materials (blue) start with considerably reduced emissions. Ambitious energy-efficiency modernizations of old buildings (red dashed line) achieve an only slightly

existing building stock could be effectively utilized [6]. He describes 50 tools to make better use of buildings, ranging from the traditional change of use right up to concepts for cataloging and managing empty stock. Fuhrhop also highlights the considerable quantities of grey energy contained in existing buildings, which would be lost for future use and destroyed upon demolition. In addition, he points out the ecological potential concealed in their function, because existing buildings are often used inefficiently purely due to their internal organisation.

With initiatives across Germany and the 2020 exhibition and publication, "Sorge um den Bestand" (Concern for the Existing Stock), the Bund Deutscher Architektinnen und Architekten (Association of German Architects, BDA) together with the Deutsches Architektur Zentrum (German Centre for Architecture, DAZ) points out that building in the existing context is key to a successful transformation of construction. This highlights the necessary changes in the established decision-making processes needed for a substantial revaluation of the buildings we already have at our disposal [7]. The fundamental analysis of the systematic retention and further use of buildings instead of demolishing and replacing them with new structures also considers the social and economic questions that would accompany such a paradigm change. This will require not least a fundamental shift in thinking by all actors, from clients and designers to contractors and building users. Legal, commercial, financial and insurance aspects often present greater obstacles to achieving a fair comparison or even preclude ecological considerations. Regional chambers of architects with the backing of various professional associations therefore request a "renovation ordinance", which would involve rewriting the federal model build-

ing regulations and the building regulations of each German federal state to have them focus primarily on building in existing stock rather than on the requirements for new construction.

In fact, from an ecological viewpoint, nothing makes more sense than avoiding new construction whenever existing buildings can be converted and continue to be used instead. Existing stock has potential that can be realized by more efficient use of residential space (above all, detached and semi-detached houses), while the conversion of empty offices or similar buildings can quickly contribute to the current and serious shortage of housing without the lead times associated with new construction. In addition to making the most of this sufficiency potential through the appropriate use of existing stock, an energy-efficiency refurbishment is essential in most cases to achieve an ecologically effective reuse that would enable the largely climate-neutral or even climate-positive future operation of buildings.

Spatial sufficiency and energy efficiency – neither makes any sense without the other. Since the post-war era, the energy required for heating per square metre of floor area in Germany has been reduced by efficiency gains from 240 kWh/m²a to 150 kWh/m²a. However, the energy required for heating per capita has hardly changed over the same period. This is explained by the average living space per capita having more than doubled due to continual growth since the 1960s to 2.3 times its former value [8].

Existing stock for more efficiency

Of all the requirements currently imposed on the existing stock considering the acute housing shortage and by the need to build more sustainably,

none is more pressing than achieving higher energy efficiency, densification and change of use. Of course, other specific requirements, such as fire safety, barrier-free access, contaminant remediation or future maintenance greatly influence what can be done with existing architecture. However, the effects of requirements in relation to building typology, building use, construction system, building services and aesthetics are much less extensive. This is largely due to legislation: since 2002 the German Energy Conservation Act and Ordinance (and today the German Buildings Energy Act, GEG) have required compliance with ever-stricter minimum values for building components modified beyond the scope of maintenance measures. The consequence is that any intervention in the building fabric becomes a potential energy-efficiency modernization. The European Union's Energy Performance of Buildings Directive (EPBD 2023), which was adopted in March 2023 in the European Parliament, further provides that the most energy-inefficient buildings in every EU member state (in accordance with national energy-efficiency classes A to G) must be updated to a more efficient standard by modernization. Public buildings and private commercial non-residential buildings must have an efficiency class of at least E by the beginning of 2027 and achieve efficiency class D before the beginning of 2030. The deadline for residential buildings is three years later in each case. Although the directive can still be influenced by the member states, the principal geopolitical aim is clear: Europe is to become more resilient and independent of non-European energy suppliers. This is, on the one hand, one of the lessons to be drawn from the Russian war of aggression against Ukraine, in which Europe was open to blackmail as

Simone Rosenberg

less efficient energy standard than new construction; however, they start with considerably less emissions. Old buildings modernized using biogenic building materials (blue dashed line) with their stored CO_2, begin the life cycle analysis with negative emissions and create the lowest total emissions for the first decades.
2   Energy-efficiency refurbishment and conversion using biogenic building materials, detached house, Munich (DE) 2012, Ruth Klingelhöfer-Krötsch und Stefan Krötsch
3   Options for modernizing an existing building

2

a result of its dependence on Russian energy suppliers. On the other hand, this is a logical and effective step on the way to self-defined and internationally agreed European and national climate goals. The EU directive has resulted in gigantic pressure to renovate. As an outcome, one half of all the buildings in Germany will require to be at least partially modernized by 2030.

These and other regulations reflect the fact that the energy savings to be achieved in the existing stock, which is responsible for 42 % of the energy Europe consumes and 36 % of its greenhouse emissions [9], are the most important contribution to the energy transition. Although the political discussion and the financial subsidization are mainly concerned with the generation of electricity, the actual hope lies in increasing the efficiency of buildings. Important areas of the industry and freight transport need to compete on global levels. Therefore, they are elusive to direct intervention by national governments. As a result, huge expectations lie in the building sector. In Germany, the stock from the period of reconstruction after the Second World War has a key role to play because just under half of the buildings in Germany were built between 1949 and 1978 [10]. At the same time, the plain render facades of this type of architecture are seen to have much more potential for installing facade insulation than the often more richly decorated exterior walls of older buildings.

No other application than facade insulation leads to disagreements that can hardly be reconciled between those in favour of and those in opposition to the energy efficient modernization of buildings. This is no surprise because facades are not merely parts of buildings; they largely define and shape our public space.

Meanwhile, the ecological difficulties and differences of approaches are nowhere so apparent as in the retrofitting of insulation to external walls. A good example of this is the ongoing discussion on rendered external thermal insulation composite systems (ETICS), the by far most often used product for the energy-efficiency refurbishment of exterior walls in Germany since the 1970s. The insulation thicknesses and details (connections to windows and other building components) of these systems have been continually further developed since then and modified to meet each new change in the requirements for energy efficiency (Fig. 4, p. 10). Compared to other methods of exterior wall renovation (e.g. with suspended, rear-ventilated facade cladding), they are certainly well ahead of the competition when it comes to manufacturing costs. However, they hold some significant disadvantages: they are less robust in terms of building physics, comparatively more prone to damage, difficult to repair, and hard to dispose of. The disposal of plastic-based external thermal insulation composite systems in particular presents a huge problem for the future.

Architectural quality

For existing buildings, the installation of external insulation not only means losing their original exterior materiality but also architectural proportions. This is the case especially for architecture built during the period of reconstruction after the Second World War, which is characterized less by elaborate ornamentation and more by a sensitive aptness and plain, but not banal, architectural features. These are related to the construction type and coincide with a loss of identity. Laypeople are often unaware

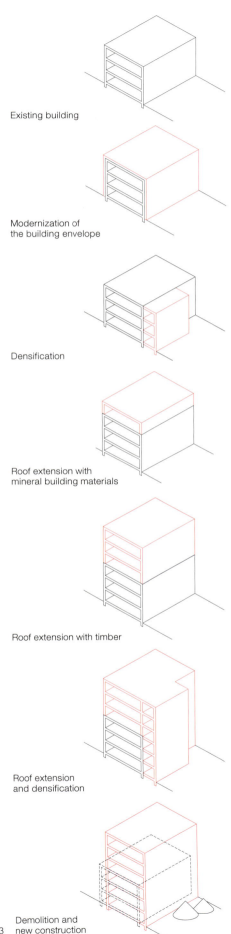

Existing building

Modernization of
the building envelope

Densification

Roof extension with
mineral building materials

Roof extension with timber

Roof extension
and densification

3   Demolition and
new construction

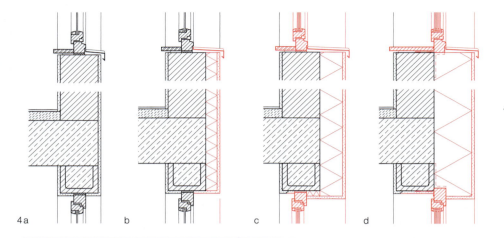

4a   b   c   d

4   Typical exterior wall construction for energy-efficiency modernizations of existing post-war modernist buildings with ETICS according to the statutory requirements for the thermal transmittance of exterior walls at the time of construction
   a   Initial situation: building materials with high thermal transmittance; the construction features thermal bridges along slab edges and window lintels as a result of the material used (reinforced concrete)
   b   Modernization from the 1970s: polystyrene

Material cycle:

Wood is intrinsically a recyclable and carbon-neutral construction material. If wood is sent for thermal recovery at the end of its service life or is allowed to rot, the greater part of its material substance is released as CO_2. This CO_2 can be metabolized via photosynthesis again into wood, which can then be used once more. Hence the material is normally considered as almost climate-neutral in the life cycle analysis. If wood as a building material is not mixed with additional substances (e.g. glue, varnish, paint, preservatives), it is a fully recyclable material. In the light of the climate crisis, however, it is very worthwhile to retain the CO_2 stored in the wood for as long as possible and prevent its release, in order to relieve the climate system over the long term. This can happen primarily in three ways:
1. Recycling of the material: use of old wood for manufacturing new wood-based materials (e.g. OSB board, chipboard)
2. The reuse of complete building components (walls, ceilings, columns, beams etc.)
3. Retention of whole buildings by prolonged use or change of use

The reuse of old wood (see 1) is functional and practical, but usually results in low-grade reuse (downcycling) and in it being mixed with additional substances (glue etc.). Building in existing stock (see 3) is an important part of architecture and the most important module of the transformation of the use of resources in the construction industry in Europe. Since the approach has long been an important part of traditional practice, there are clearly established guidelines for how to deal with old building components and materials. On the other hand, the reuse of complete building components is for the most part unclear in Germany with respect to its technical and legal implementation (see 2). However, at the same time, this has great potential because the use of complete building components usually enables an equally valuable exploitation of the material and, in the case of wood, a complete retention of the stored CO_2.

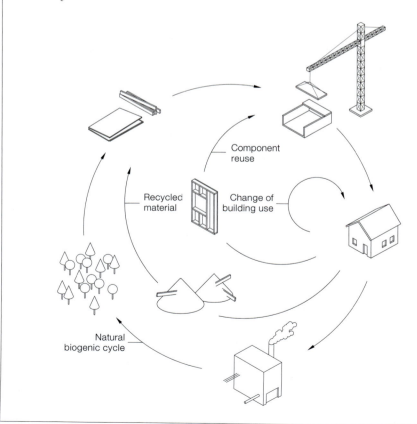

Recycled material

Component reuse

Change of building use

Natural biogenic cycle

of this and the topic is seldom publicly discussed.. The success of the energy transition depends on its long-term, broad acceptance. All the more astonishing, therefore, that the architectural design of energy-efficient building refurbishments is rarely embraced as an opportunity or as socially relevant task by either architects or clients. In most cases, an architectural practice is not involved; the design is often based on a calculation of the energy demand or undertaken using building component insulation values derived from tables in the latest guidance documents. This approach makes the modernization goals seen to be necessary a matter of compliance with standards or at best something to be determined by engineering calculations. The idea that modernization measures are important aspects of architecture remains knowingly or unknowingly unrecognized.

Detached from all the other aspects of architecture, a facade insulation project not only has considerable potential to destroy architectural value; the added value it creates may also be dubious. This becomes apparent as the increasingly documented performance gap when buildings do not achieve the forecast savings after modernization. Energy efficiency is not a purely technical issue but considerably more dependent on how the building users identify with the modernization goals and how they operate the building. Unless the refurbishment goes beyond purely technical measures and results in a systematic, synergetic improvement, the buildings or their correct operation will remain misunderstood and moreover lose their architectural balance. Although not recognizable at first glance nor measurable in numbers, architectural identity is essential for the lasting acceptance of a building.

Notes
[1] Order of the first Senat of the Ferderal Constitutional Court of 24 March 2021 – 1 BvR 2656/18 – 1 BvR 78/20 – 1 BvR 96/20 – 1 BvR 288/20
[2] dena-Gebäudereport 2022, p. 55
[3] Umweltbundesamt 12/2023: www.umweltbundesamt.de/daten/ressourcen-abfall/rohstoffe-als-ressource/gesamter-materialaufwand-deutschlands
[4] Umweltbundesamt 12/2023: www.umweltbundesamt.de/daten/ressourcen-abfall/abfallaufkommen
[5] Umweltbundesamt 12/2023: www.umweltbundesamt.de/daten/umweltindikatoren/indikator-energieverbrauch-fuer-gebaeude
[6] Fuhrhop, Daniel: Verbietet das Bauen! Eine Streitschrift. Munich 2015
[7] Bahner, Olaf; Böttger, Matthias; Holzberg, Laura: Sorge um den Bestand – Zehn Strategien für die Architektur. Berlin 2020
[8] BMWi: Forschung für eine umweltschonende, zuverlässige und bezahlbare Energieversorgung. Munich 2011, p. 29
[9] Energy Performance of Buildings Directive. https://energy.ec.europa.eu/topics/energy-efficiency/energy-efficient-buildings/energy-performance-buildings-directive_en; date 12/2023
[10] Arbeitsgemeinschaft Energiebilanzen 10/2012, BMWi
[11] Petzet, Muck et al.: Konservieren – Interpretieren – Transformieren: Erhalten, Deuten und Wandeln von Bauten der Jahre 1950 bis 1975. Bayerische Architektenkammer. Akademie für Fort- und Weiterbildung. Munich 2014

or mineral fibre insulation (ca. 6 cm) with design-related thermal bridges along window reveal connections
c Modernization from the 1990s: insulation (approx. 12 cm) and window replacement; design-related thermal bridge along window sill due to setting window into wall opening
d Contemporary modernization: insulation (approx. 20 cm), window replacement; design-related thermal bridges due to setting window into opening in the insulation layer and minimal frame insulation overlap

Projects in which an energy-efficiency modernization or the achievement of other technical or organisational requirements was regarded as an opportunity for rethinking the overall structure of the building in order to implement fundamental adjustments and improvements are the ones that turn out to be convincing, even groundbreaking. The same applies to projects that seize the opportunity to further develop existing buildings also with respect to their architectural expression and their spatial qualities in which the architecture is precisely analyzed and "conserved, interpreted or transformed" based on their characteristics [11]. This is because the need for an energy-efficiency modernization always coincides with the opportunity for extension, which symbolizes a point of departure into the new on the basis of the old.

Potential of timber in existing stock

The mass of a timber building is only 20–50% of one consisting of mineral construction materials. At around 80 N/mm², structural timber has a much lower tensile strength (compressive strength ca. 75 N/mm²) than construction steel at about 370 N/mm². However, since the weight of wood is only about 1/16 that of steel, wood offers a considerably better self-weight to strength ratio (by a factor of about 2). This allows extensive prefabrication of large and complex components, optimization of the design and manufacturing process, drastically reduced time on site and maximum construction precision. The light weight of wood is a particular advantage for building in existing stock:
• Timber is eminently suitable for adding storeys to buildings because the load capacity reserves of existing buildings can be optimally utilized. More storeys can be added with timber structures than with mineral construction materials.
• Prefabricated elements can be attached to existing buildings in a relatively simple manner for purposes of renovating components such as floors, walls or roofs.
• A high degree of prefabrication enables the shortest of construction times and minimizes the use of urban infrastructure and adverse impacts on building residents and occupants.

Timber has another advantage in particular for energy-efficiency refurbishments of existing stock: it has the lowest thermal conductivity of all load-bearing construction materials. The load-bearing structure can be built into the insulation layer without resulting in significant thermal bridges, which allows the building components to be very compact. The footprint of frame wall construction is only 3/4 that of comparable masonry construction. In towns and cities, this has great potential for improved utilization of valuable, limited building space.
Changing and prolonging the use of the existing stock is one of the most important tasks for the "Bauwende", the ecological transformation of the construction sector. The manner and means of the renovation or construction work are crucial for their acceptance and the actual life cycle analysis. Existing buildings must also demonstrate the capacity for efficient future operation and for achieving meaningful urban density. Last but not least, architectural quality plays a crucial role in how we treat our architectural heritage. In order to prevent a boomerang effect, the building stock must exhibit overall carbon-neutral operation and adaptability to meet the needs of future generations. From an ecological point of view, only renewable and circular material and energy flows may be used.

Timber and other biogenic building materials therefore complement existing building stock in an ideal way. With respect to the Global Warming Potential (GWP), they have the unique capacity of actively relieving the impact on the climate: they store considerably more CO_2 from the atmosphere than they cause from their manufacture. Despite this fact, new timber construction that stores more CO_2 than it emits overall remains unusual, since every new timber construction also requires a large quantity of non-renewable raw materials. In terms of life cycle analysis, the majority of buildings contain reinforced concrete components, which are certainly unavoidable for the lower floors and perhaps also for the stairwells. When building in existing stock, timber is a material with an unmistakable ecological potential, because almost every existing building structure already contains the components in contact with the ground, the foundations and most of the circulation areas. In addition, these buildings are typically sited with access to existing urban and public utility infrastructure. Timber construction is therefore able to contribute in the best way it possibly could: with building components primarily made from biogenic materials, which are superior to conventional construction materials according to all life cycle analysis indicators. Combining the extensive retention of existing building stock and the use of timber and other biogenic construction materials for the necessary renovation, conversion and increase in urban density is the optimum precondition for a real change towards climate protection in building.

Life Cycle Assessment in Timber Construction and Existing Stock

Thomas Stark

In the construction industry, the concept of life cycle assessment (LCA) is used to calculate, categorize and specify all environmental impacts arising in connection with the building materials used, in addition to determining the energy consumption during operation, which has been the typical focus up to now. The methodology for life cycle assessment is defined by the standards DIN EN ISO 14040 to 14044 [1], but in practice there is ample scope for more specific calculations. The most important definition is the reference study period, commonly considered to be the total life cycle of a building, which, in an ideal case, comprises everything from the extraction of the raw material, construction and repair during operation to its potential demolition. For this purpose, the standard defines four time periods, life cycle stages A to D, which are each subdivided into modules (Fig. 1). A period of 50 years is suggested for the use stage B. The scope of the LCA and the building elements considered – from the structural frame to the detail of the interior finishes – as well as the choice of material datasets can be set to suit each study. For this reason, the results of different life cycle assessments are not always directly comparable and must always be considered in context of the LCA system boundary.

A further important aspect in the calculation of a life cycle assessment is the choice of impact categories. These quantify the direct effect on the earth's ecosystem. The standard contains over 40 impact categories. However, the category Global Warming with the parameter Global Warming Potential (GWP) measured as CO_2 equivalent has emerged as the dominant indicator. Given as a mass in grams, kilograms or tonnes, this parameter is the most explicit measure of the direct impact on the global greenhouse effect and the associated warming

of the climate, which is currently ranked as the greatest challenge facing the whole world. The main cause of the emission of CO_2 lies in the use of fossil energy sources (non-renewable resources) for the production of construction materials. Therefore, this is usually calculated and reported in the impact category Primary Energy non-Renewable – Total (PENRT). In the past, life cycle assessments were mainly applied within the scope of pilot and research projects. In the meantime, however, well-founded and freely accessible databases (e.g. Ökobaudat) for a multitude of construction materials as well as suitable software tools (e.g. eLCA) have become available to enable life cycle assessment to become a useful means of auditing (e.g. DGNB, BNB) [2].

Reuse of existing buildings in LCAs

Up to now, the focus of life cycle assessment has been on the evaluation of different material concepts in new buildings. However, in principle, the method can also be used to include the embodied energy, often referred to as grey energy, and the grey emissions in the planning of projects involving the reuse of existing buildings. Knowledge of embodied grey energy allows identifying the quantity of energy and the associated CO_2 emissions originally caused in the manufacture and construction of the existing buildings. Because no suitable database exists for the earlier construction measures, it is helpful to calculate the above values based on what would be involved by manufacturing and constructing a contemporary building of comparable mass. Retaining a building or elements of the building secures its further use, prevents the loss of energy expended and avoids the energy consumption otherwise caused

1 Life cycle stages A to D of a building in accordance with DIN EN 15978:2012-10
2 Comparison of greenhouse gas emissions of mineral-based and biogenic building materials in the life cycle assessment based on the example of concrete class C20/25, hollow building blocks and glued laminated softwood timber, per 1 m³ volume

Building life cycle

A Production and construction	B Use	C Disposal	D Advantages and loads beyond the system boundaries
A1 Raw material supply A2 Transport A3 Manufacturing A4 Transport A5 Construction/ installation	B1 Use B2 Maintenance B3 Repair B4 Replacement B5 Refurbishment B6 Operational energy use B7 Operational water use	C1 Deconstruction/ demolition C2 Transport C3 Waste processing C4 Disposal	D Reuse, recovery and recycling potential

according to DIN EN 15978

1

by constructing a new building. This effect can be quantified in a transparent manner only through a life cycle assessment and would otherwise remain "invisible". This life cycle methodology has, up to now, been rarely used in practice, however, it should become the rule. Building elements in contact with the earth and large primary constructions made from mineral materials represent a huge and worthwhile potential in terms of their embodied energy, which can be taken advantage of only by their retention. Partial reuse of existing building elements within new construction projects is currently taken into account in life cycle assessments by assigning zero emissions to these elements, which has a positive effect in the overall assessment of new buildings. For new construction unrelated to building in an existing context, no consideration is given to whether an existing structure was demolished or not in the course of realizing the new project. Thus, there is need for revision. Equally, the life cycle assessment does not consider what the preconditions for a later continuation or new use would be for the construction of a building (e.g. the possibility and amount of work involved in separating the demolished building into single types of materials).

In the long term, the assessment of the elements of existing buildings on the basis of non-renewable primary energy or CO_2 emissions also has the disadvantage that the "ecological value" of the existing building stock will steadily decrease as the energy transition progresses and the database values improve. For an adequate evaluation of a positive environmental impact, it would be helpful to include the impact category "abiotic resource expenditure". Thus far, this exemplary category has received little attention. It is highly suitable to illustrate the valuation of long-term use of existing

(and, to a major degree, mineral) stock.. This parameter can measure the non-renewable material flows in construction, which unfortunately is still not adequately weighted in the life cycle assessment. This is another example of a necessary correction required here in order to better depict the impacts with respect to extraction of raw materials from the earth and the generation of waste. The retention of building stock in conjunction with the use of biogenic building materials represents the key strategy in this situation.

Special aspects of the building material wood in LCAs

Wood is the most important example of biogenic raw materials. In contrast to all other construction materials (mineral products, metals, plastics, glass etc.), biogenic substances behave in a fundamentally different way, above all with respect to CO_2 emissions: With non-biogenic building materials, almost all the CO_2 emissions arise directly during the manufacturing process and are already in the atmosphere by the time the building is complete. In contrast, biogenic (renewable) construction materials absorb CO_2

as they grow, which remains locked within the relevant building component for the whole period of its use. Therefore, the balance timeframe of the life cycle assessment is crucially important: if the focus is exclusively on the manufacture and construction of the building, then the calculation for biogenic building materials results in negative CO_2 emissions, because their use as a building component prevents their natural decay and the associated release of CO_2 into the atmosphere. The building functions as a CO_2 store, which is greater the more biogenic mass it contains. In an eco-balance, the entire life cycle tends to be considered and thus, a so-called end-of-life scenario needs to be defined. It is typically assumed that biogenic materials will be subject to thermal recovery once the life cycle terminates. In such cases, the CO_2 bound within the substance is completely released into the atmosphere. For renewable construction materials, the total figure related to bound CO_2 thus results only in a neutral balance. Although an energy credit can be calculated to compensate for the CO_2, using the recycling potential in module D, this proportion is small and is usually not taken into account in the assessment. Instead, it is highlighted separately, since stage D

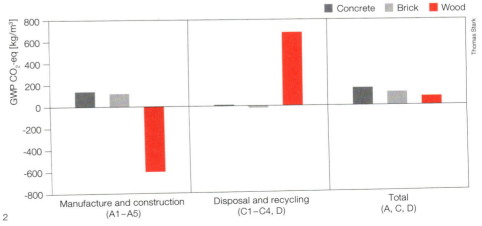

2

3   Installation of a solid timber floor in a multistorey
    apartment building
4   Adding a timber storey to a building consisting
    of mineral-based materials
5   Aspects of biogenic building materials in the
    life cycle assessment with respect to the timing
    of the CO_2 emissions and the future options for
    action

and thus, module D are formally defined as external to the life cycle of the building under assessment. In addition, fossil energy sources are used for harvesting and processing for the manufacture of the biogenic materials, with the result that wood-based building components would also lead to CO_2 emissions, even if module D were included in a current life cycle assessment (Fig. 2, p. 13). These emissions relate to the individual component and are clearly smaller than, for example, those of mineral-based materials. In the life cycle assessment as a whole for building components in contact with the earth, windows, building services equipment etc., the outcome of a life cycle assessment for typical timber buildings is often only slightly better than that of a traditional solid construction made of masonry or concrete. This is a further argument for retaining existing stock, because demolishing and replacing buildings consumes considerably more resources and creates more emissions over the life cycle even if the new buildings were primarily made of timber.

Alternative end-of-life scenarios for biogenic building materials

The result of a life cycle assessment involving a high proportion of wooden materials is – as explained in the section above – considerably influenced by which end-of-life scenario is adopted. The standard scenario of thermal recovery is the current basis for all life cycle assessment calculations in accordance with the auditing processes (DGNB, BNB etc.) as well as for the calculation in accordance with the Quality Seal for Sustainable Buildings (QNG), which forms part of the German federal government's funding strategy. This largely

corresponds to current building practice. However, applying the status quo to scenarios of events projected to happen 50 years from now isn't necessarily sensible, given this is the typical reference study period for a life cycle assessment. From today's point of view, it is quite conceivable, for example, that thermal recovery of biogenic building materials from demolition may be prohibited in the future. The options then would be to reuse them as building materials or to permanently sequester their CO_2 by carbon capture and storage (CCS), with the latter likely to be considerably easier to implement, since trials are currently conducted with flue gas emissions. A suitable regulation would then ensure that the CO_2 bound in timber building components is permanently removed from the atmosphere (Fig. 5). Certainly, this type of scenario considerably improves the life cycle assessment of timber buildings. The permanent storage of CO_2 allows building with biogenic materials to act as a kind of "repair" of the earlier combustion of fossil resources. This is also the idea behind the published thesis of the climate researcher Hans Joachim Schellnhuber: "We could build ourselves out of the climate crisis." [3] The approach of maximizing carbon storage requires an evaluation of the advantages of efficient resource use also for biogenic materials. The less material is used for a specific function, the more the potential of biogenic materials as substitute for mineral-based materials increases.
A further important factor in this context is the disadvantageous circumstance that the timing of the CO_2 emissions has no relevance in the assessment. The emissions across all the life cycle stages are totalled into one sum, without any consideration of when they occur. This can make a significant difference: on

the one hand, it is completely relevant whether the emissions occur at the beginning of the life cycle assessment and then can impact the atmosphere 50 years later or whether they do not enter the atmosphere until the end of the life cycle. Above all, however, this difference results in shifting the responsibility: with non-biogenic building materials, the emissions occur immediately at the time of the manufacture and construction of the building and are the responsibility of the designers. With biogenic building materials, the designers organize the storage of the CO_2 bound in those materials. Future generations, in the event of demolition, can choose whether and to what extent the bound emissions are released into the atmosphere (Fig. 3).

Quality features of the database

To judge the validity of a life cycle assessment, it is also relevant to know which data the calculations are based on, and how large any deviations from them may potentially turn out to be in practice. As with the energy performance assessment for building operation, flat rate indicators are required to allow the calculations to be completed without unreasonable effort. For assessments in accordance with the German Buildings Energy Act (GEG), designers can draw on many decades of practical experience using the earlier Energy Conservation Ordinance (EnEV) and Thermal Insulation Ordinances (WSV). However, there are some considerable differences between the figures for theoretical demand and real consumption. This applies in particular to the life cycle assessment because there are great differences in the validity of the individual modules: the results of the product and construction process stage A (in particular modules A1–A3)

4

are based on actual design data and calculations of masses. They are therefore relatively valid in conjunction with the indicators from the current databases. The use stage (modules B) also provides good estimates, but the above-mentioned uncertainties make them less reliable, because they are based on scenarios of the future. The calculations for the demolition phase are a completely different story. This phase is an entirely fictional scenario. In terms of the scheduling of and the expenditure for a potential demolition and the way of dealing with related materials, its likelihood of occurring as planned can be considered very low. From today's perspective, defining the environmental boundary conditions for a time 50 years in the future must be viewed as a highly speculative undertaking. However, in accordance with typical practice, all the partial results of the individual modules are given equal weight in the total indicator. As discussed in "Special aspects of the

material wood in LCAs" (p. 13f.), revising these aspects appears to be prudent (Fig. 5), particularly with respect to the importance of using biogenic building materials.

General recommendations

On the basis of these deliberations, the following general strategy from the point of view of life cycle assessments can be derived:
• The retention and prolonged use of existing buildings incorporating mineral-based materials or their primary construction components (in particular those in contact with the ground) is always more advantageous in all impact categories of the life cycle assessment than demolition and replacement with new buildings, particularly with regard to the consumption of abiotic resources in the long term.

• Also advantageous would be replacement or retrofit measures within the existing stock, provided they were constructed as much as possible from biogenic building materials.

In this respect, it is possible to formulate a general recommendation in terms of life cycle assessment that the existing building stock should be preserved as far as possible in conjunction with the use of biogenic building materials.

Notes
[1] The principle of life cycle assessment is defined in the international ISO standards 14040:2006 and 14044:2006 and implemented in the German standards (DIN EN ISO 14040, DIN EN ISO 14044). This is supplemented for the construction field by DIN EN 15978 Sustainability of construction works - Assessment of environmental performance of buildings - Calculation method.
[2] Ökobaudat: www.oekobaudat.de, eLCA: www.bauteileditor.de, DGNB: www.dgnb.de, BNB: www.bnb-nachhaltigesbauen.de
[3] Schellnhuber, Hans Joachim, et al. in: "Können wir uns aus der Klimakrise herausbauen?", presentation at ProHolz Oberösterreich, 2020

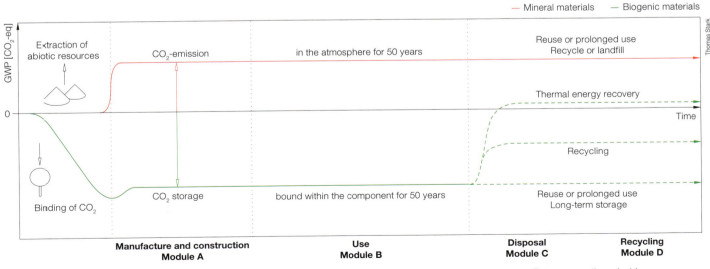

5

Fire Protection in Timber Construction

Thomas Engel

Combustibility

Although timber is the most important renewable raw material of the future, it is also a combustible building material. Irrespective of this, all required fire resistance ratings can also be achieved with wood by suitably dimensioning members or cladding the building component. The critical factor for the design in this case is charring. When exposed to fire, wood forms a charring layer, which acts as a protective coating. This charring delays combustion of the remainder of the cross section because the protective coating layer slows the inward progress of thermal decomposition. Among other things, this is due to the lower thermal conductivity of the charcoal and the wood. In related standards, the boundary temperature between the charring layer and the non-burnt cross section (char-line) is specified as 300 °C in EN 1995-1-2. The burning limit is defined as the region with no carbonization but a brown colouration (Fig. 1).

Charring behaviour

One of the important parameters in the assessment of the load-bearing capability of timber components exposed to fire is the charring rate. The charring rate β is defined as the speed at which timber is transformed into charcoal. The residual cross section for any fire duration can be calculated using the charring rate and taking into account the occurring charring phases.

The approach to fire design given in EN 1995-1-2 for solid wood assumes a constant charring rate, which ranges from 0.65 to 0.8 mm/min, depending on the type of wood and the scenario. This model can be applied to solid wood, dowel laminated timber (DLT) compo-

nents and typically also to glued laminated timber (GLT).

The charring model for cross-laminated timber (CLT) can, on the other hand, deviate from the above-described constant-rate approach and be influenced by the product-specific properties and installation situation. Cross-laminated timber consists of several layers of timber laminated crosswise to the one below. Unlike the situation with glued laminated timber and solid timber components, the adhesive layer runs parallel to the charring and hence parallel to the charcoal layer (Fig. 2). The thermal behaviour of the adhesive surface bonding, the dimensioning of the timber lamellae, the element composition, and the orientation of the components determine the charring behaviour of cross-laminated timber. The generally valid concept of constant burnout rate is not principally applicable. In fact, it is only applicable to cross laminated timber for which the thermal behavior of the surface bonding is evaluated as equivalent to solid timber [1].

Fire tests show that the carbonized timber lamellae can fall off, with the consequence that the protective function of the charring layer ("protective coating") is lost for the underlying cross section. For a while, this leads to an increased charring rate (phase 2 on Fig. 4b), until an adequately thick charring layer (25 mm) has formed [2]. One of the main reasons for the protective charring layers falling off is the limited thermal resistance of the adhesive layer between the individual timber lamellae in the event of fire.

Due to the orientation of the component and the force of gravity, this form of disintegration is more pronounced with cross-laminated timber ceiling components than with cross-laminated timber walls of the same layer construction [3].

1 Burning limit with the associated temperature gradients
2 Charring behaviour of dowel laminated timber (DLT) or glued laminated timber (GLT) and cross-laminated timber (CLT)
3 Comparison of the protective effects of claddings in accordance with EN 1995-1-2 and EN 13501-2
4 Charring phases for unprotected cross-laminated timber building components, if
  a the glued surfaces have no influence on the charring performance,
  b the glued surfaces have an influence on the charring performance. Phase 1 = normal charring or consolidated charring, after which the charring layer has achieved a thickness of 25 mm, Phase 2 = increased charring.

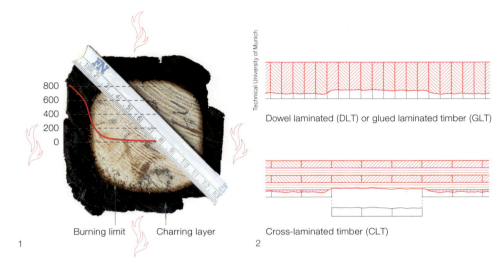

800
600
400
200
0

Burning limit   Charring layer

1

Dowel laminated (DLT) or glued laminated timber (GLT)

Cross-laminated timber (CLT)

2

Technical University of Munich

Efficacy of fire protection cladding

Cladding timber elements plays a significant role in the fire design of timber components and constructions. Cladding not only defines the appearance of component surfaces, it also has a positive influence on their performance in the case of a fire. Its protective effect enables an optimum design of the timber components or may even prevent them from contributing to a fire event. The materials used for cladding are mainly non-combustible drywall construction products such as gypsum board, gypsum fibreboard, calcium silicate or clay boards. Depending on the field of application and regulations, different terms are used in practice to describe these types of cladding, a phenomenon which can be attributed to previously different fire protection goals or lack of knowledge on the part of the designers. For example, terms used include fire-protection cladding, cladding with fire protection ability, encapsulation cladding or protection cladding, among many others.

The precise definition and consistent denomination of the cladding type plays a crucial role, particularly for its use in multistorey timber construction, if the desired protective function is to be provided for the timber building component. The protective ability of these cladding systems is defined by the material characteristics of the cladding, its installation and construction details (thickness, connection type, joint formation, backing material).

In terms of protective effect, there are two types of cladding. In addition to cladding with a classified fire protection function (cladding with effective fire protection abbreviation K_2 based on EN 13501-2), there is also fire protection cladding in accordance with EN 1995-1-2,

abbreviation t_{ch}. Fig. 3 shows a comparison of the protection functions of both cladding types.

Special aspects of German building regulations

Due to the federal system in Germany, there are 16 sets of building regulations, one for each of the German states. These building regulations differ from one another to a greater or lesser extent. The permissibility of use of timber as a combustible building material depends on the building type and is regulated in the

relevant state building regulations. Fortunately, as a result of a process of amendment in all 16 federal states that started in 2015 in Baden-Württemberg, building components made from combustible construction materials have been permitted for buildings with more than three and up to nine above-ground storeys (building classes 4 & 5, see section Building classes p. 62ff.), provided that additional requirements and measures are met. As a result, in accordance with the respective state building regulations of all 16 federal states, "regulated" timber constructions can be erected up to the highrise limit.

Assessment criterion	Cladding with fire protection ability in accordance with DIN EN 13501-2 (abbr.: K_2)	Protection cladding in accordance with DIN EN 1995 1-2 (abbr. t_{ch})
Limit of the temperature (increase) behind the cladding	Temperature increase above the initial temperature • average no more than 250 K • maximum no more than 270 K	The boundary temperature for t_{ch} (start of charring) is 300 °C
Exclusion of burnt or carbonized material behind the cladding	Also in the area of the means of attachment and joints (visual evaluation after the end of the test)	Only in the surface areas (joints are considered separately, means of attachment are not taken into account)
Falling off of cladding	Falling off or disintegration (even in parts) is not permissible.	Time elapsed until cladding falls off with reduced charring behind it is referred to as t_f

3

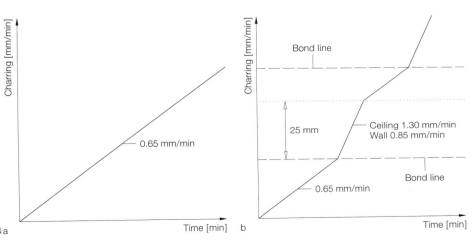

4a   b

5   Multistorey timber building, Prinz-Eugen-Park
    (WA14 Ost), Munich (DE) 2020, ARGE Architektur-
    Werkstatt Vallentin GmbH, Johannes Kaufmann
    Architektur
6   Various types of cladding for wooden facades
7   Overview of various types of construction of
    wooden facades for a refurbished existing building

The model guidelines (M-HFHHolzR) concerning fire design requirements for timber frame wall components [4] from 2004 allowed regulated (without departures) multistorey structures to be built from timber for the first time in Germany. The model guidelines limited this use to buildings (building class (GK) 4, see section Building classes p. 62ff.). The requirement to form load-bearing, stiffening or fire-separating construction components with a fire resistance rating of (REI) 60 $K_2$60 is fulfilled with non-combustible

insulation and a cladding with fire protection ability (K_2, see Fig. 4, p. 17). Cladding with fire protection ability has the task of protecting the combustible timber building component from fire for a period of 60 minutes. In the past, many buildings, mostly housing, were erected in this manner (Fig. 5).

Visible timber surfaces, the use of engineered wood products (e.g. cross- or glued laminated timber) or load-bearing building components made of timber were not permitted according to these

guidelines in buildings with five to nine storeys (high-rise limit) above ground (building class (GK) 5, see section Building classes p. 62ff.). This changed with the new model guideline concerning fire design requirements for building components and external wall cladding in timber construction (MHolzBauRL) [5], which was first published in 2021 by the expert committee building authority of the Conference of Building Ministers. The content of the current guideline is principally divided into the regulations concerning:

*   Requirements of building components in timber frame and frame wall construction
*   Requirements of building components constructed in solid timber
*   Requirements of wooden facades for fire safety

In the light of the data from the research project TIMpuls [6], the current omission of timber frame and frame wall construction from consideration for use in buildings with five to nine storeys above ground is no longer justifiable from a fire protection perspective. This federal research project by the Technical University of Munich, Technical University of Braunschweig, Magdeburg-Stendal University of Applied Sciences and the Institute of Fire and Civil Protection Heyrothsberge studied fire design issues of multistorey timber buildings with the goal of further developing building control regulations for the wider use of timber construction. According to the research, there are no obstacles to designing the relevant building components and connections for a fire resistance of 90 minutes, provided that the construction rules in MHolzBauRL are suitably modified and adopted for buildings with a height up to the high-rise building limit. The applicability of timber frame wall construction in these buildings will be reconsidered in

Cladding type	Schematic	Orientation	
Wood-based panels		Horizontal or vertical	
Form-fit paneling and cladding Tongue and groove profile		Horizontal	Closed facades
		Vertical	
Force-fit paneling and cladding		Horizontal	
		Vertical	
Open cladding Strip cladding Cover cladding Inverting cladding Cover strip cladding		Horizontal	Open facades
		Vertical	

6

the next amendment of MHolzBauRL [7]. Based on the tests carried out, it was also apparent that joints in timber frame wall construction can be viewed in principle as the equivalent of those in solid timber. Joints providing the same level of safety in fire can be built using timber frame wall elements. Accordingly, the new design requirements in the amended MHolzBauRL no longer explicitly differentiate between timber frame wall and solid timber construction [8].

The last part of MHolzBauRL goes into the detail of the requirements of external wooden wall cladding for buildings with more than three storeys above ground up to the high-rise building limit. The current model building regulations (MBO) issued in 2020 allow the use of normal combustible construction materials for external wall cladding on buildings with more than three storeys above ground up to the multistorey building limit. On this topic, MBO §28 (5) sentence 2 states: "[…] As a departure from clause 3, rear-ventilated external wall cladding that complies with the technical building rules in accordance with §85a, with the exception of insulation materials, is permissible with normal combustible materials." This amendment has already been adopted in many state building codes.

Fire protection for timber facades

The external wall cladding and the facade have a significant influence on the spread of fire (see "Fire protection", p. 39). In the following description of building measures for the fire design of timber facades, the term facade always relates to the building envelope. The external wall that separates the interior space of the building from the surroundings is excluded. Fig. 7 shows the facade and framing as well as the actual external wall of a

refurbished existing building. Here, the external wall consists of an existing wall component and an additional new timber frame component. The latter is typically a non-load-bearing part of the external wall. Its cladding is principally the outermost layer. It comprises visually exposed elements (such as natural stone or ceramic panels, wood siding, metal panels). These can be assembled with open, closed or overlapping joints. They are mounted onto

a frame structure and attached to the external wall by use of anchors and other connectors [9].

Types of wooden facade

Different types of timber facade constructions exist (Fig. 7). The requirements relating to weather and moisture protection have led to most wooden facades in the past being constructed as fully rear-ventilated facades. Current research shows that rear-ventilated

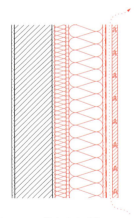

Fully rear-ventilated cladding

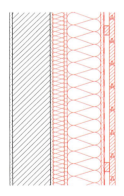

Non-rear-ventilated cladding with air cavity

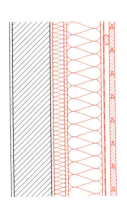

7   Partly rear-ventilated cladding

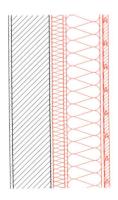

Non-rear-ventilated cladding without air cavity

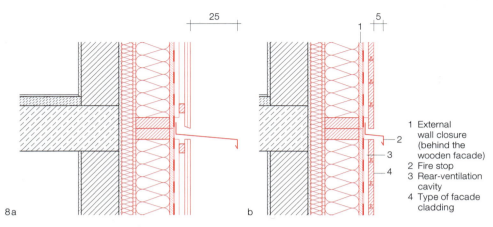

25

5
1

1 External
  wall closure
  (behind the
  wooden facade)
2 Fire stop
3 Rear-ventilation
  cavity
4 Type of facade
  cladding

8 a   b

timber facades can meet the requirements for weather and moisture protection and, as result, achieve durability
without difficulty [10]. Therefore, according to today's technical rules [11], fully
rear-ventilated, partly rear-ventilated and
to some extent non-rear-ventilated cladding with an air cavity are considered
adequate for durable, effective weather
protection.
Rear-ventilated facade cladding presents
the most critical case in relation to the
fire design of wooden facades. In comparison to non-combustible facades,
the existence of a rear-ventilation cavity
and the use of wood as a combustible
material greatly increases the spread of
fire within the rear-ventilation cavity [12].
The focus of this chapter is therefore on
the reliable fire protection design and
construction of rear-ventilated timber
facade systems.

A further important influence factor
in addition to rear-ventilation is the variety of types of cladding used for wooden
facades. Fig. 6 (p. 18) shows the cladding types commonly used in practice,
which range from closed facades (closed
facade surfaces, such as wood-based
panels) to open facades (with open joints
in the facade surfaces, such as certain
types of siding).

Principles of fire spread on timber facades
The use of timber facades requires special structural fire protection measures
to be taken to prevent or limit the spread
of fire from storey to storey across the
external wall cladding. Studies directly
comparing non-rear-ventilated and the
fully rear-ventilated wooden facades
associated with this problem come to
the conclusion that wooden cladding
with rear-ventilated cavities release twice

as much energy as wooden facade cladding without rear-ventilated cavities, which
leads to more intense flame formation and
accelerated spread of fire [13].
Horizontal fire stops that divide the continuous wooden cladding and the ventilation cavity into separate areas effectively limit the spread of fire on wooden
facades. Horizontal fire stops are created
on every floor parallel to the slab edge
and applied to the entire facade (Fig. 8,
10). The dimensions and details of the
horizontal projection in front of the facade
cladding depend primarily on the type of
facade cladding [14].
Burning of the wooden facade in the primary fire area is unavoidable and must
therefore be accepted. The vertical spread
of fire beyond the primary flame, however, must be limited because it cannot
be allowed to lead to further spread of fire
beyond the primary fire. Depending on

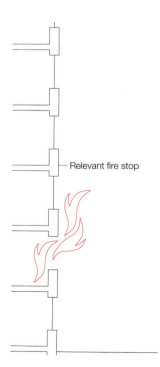

Relevant fire stop

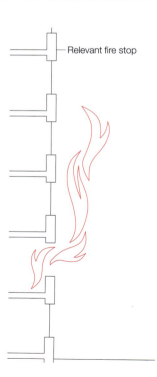

Relevant fire stop

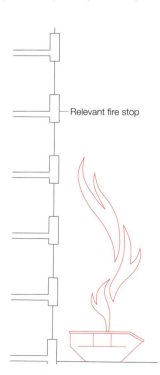

Relevant fire stop

9

the flame height, the flames can lead to flashover and reach more than one storey. The fire stop above the primary flame is the relevant measure for limiting the spread of fire (Fig. 9).

Context for fire engineering and construction of timber facades

Fig. 8b shows the typical construction of a fully rear-ventilated timber facade with all individual components and existing parts of a wooden facade – the external wall enclosure behind the wooden facade, the facade cladding, rear-ventilation cavity and the fire stop.

External wall enclosure behind a timber facade

The applied insulation material of the external insulation layer (exterior side, not interior side of the external wall) should be non-combustible. Further, to separate the timber frame wall element from the rear-ventilation layer, non-combustible cladding should be attached as outermost layer. This requirement exists because the rear-ventilation cavity is formed on one side by the wooden facade and on the other side by the outer surface of the external wall. If both surfaces were made of combustible materials, the fire would spread much more quickly within the cavity and thus reach greater heights [15]. The foil types used for weather protection or moisture management release only small amounts of heat and therefore do not significantly contribute to the spread of fire within the rear-ventilation cavity.

Type of facade cladding and rear-ventilation cavity

The technical building rules currently limit the depth of the ventilation cavity in the case of timber framing to a maximum of 50 mm (single 30 mm battens, 2 × 25 mm) cross battens [16], and in future 60 mm [17] when the design requirements in

accordance with MHolzBauRL become applicable in late 2024. The depth of the ventilation cavity (behind wooden sheathing) is typically based on the size of the battens and takes into account the practicalities of construction. Limiting the depth of the cavity to 50 mm is due to results from fire tests mostly focusing on the actual construction under observation. The quicker spread of fire within the ventilation cavity bordered by timber sheathing is not directly attributable to the increase in size of the ventilation cavity itself but rather more to construction practicalities such as how battens and crossbattens overlap or the change of orientation of the grain. From a fire safety point of view, it follows from this that even deeper ventilation cavities are technically possible [18].

With cross battens, the ventilation cavity should be closed between windows, or at least at horizontal distances of no more than 5 m by filling gaps with vertical battens in order to limit the spread of fire (Fig. 11).

Other requirements, such as how far the fire stops project, emerge from the data and depend on the cladding type of the wooden facade and the resulting fire performance (see "Fire stops", p. 22). The type of facade, in combination with the framing and the rear-ventilation cavity, greatly influences the spread of fire along

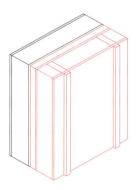

a

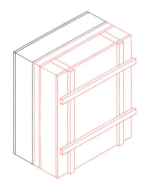

b

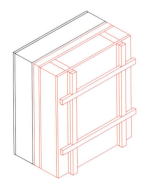

8   Schematic illustration of typical horizontal fire stops with associated depth of projection
   a Open wooden cladding
   b Tongue and groove siding
9   Various fire scenarios along the facade with relevant fire stop above the primary flame
10 Example of installed fire stops, multistorey timber building (WA 16 Ost), Prinz-Eugen-Park, Munich (DE) 2020, Dressler Mayerhofer Rössler Archi-tekten und Stadtplaner
11 Various types of battens in the framing of a wooden facade
   a Single battens
   b Cross battens
   c Double vertical battens

11 c

21

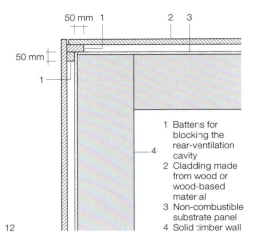

1 Battens for blocking the rear-ventilation cavity
2 Cladding made from wood or wood-based material
3 Non-combustible substrate panel
4 Solid timber wall

12

the facade [19]. The following principle applies: the more closed the facade cladding, the better the fire performance in relation to the vertical spread of fire. Moreover, the technical building rules state requirements for a minimum bulk density of ≥ 350 kg/m³ and a minimum thickness of 20 mm for wooden cladding [20]. These requirements are necessary because they significantly influence the point in time at which continuous gap formation occurs in the facade cladding due to burning in a fire event, which facilitates the spread of fire.

Particular precautions to limit the spread of fire must be taken in the design of external corners. These special measures are viewed as fulfilled if the ventilation cavity is blocked at the external corner using timber battens at least 50 mm wide (Fig. 12) [21].

Fire stops

Horizontal fire stops typically consist of sheet steel and are installed continuously over the whole width of the facade (Fig. 13, 14). As a rule, they are positioned on every storey at the transition point between storeys. They must extend to a layer of non-combustible construction materials (e.g. gypsum board or gypsum fibreboard). The required thickness of the steel sheet depends on the depth of the projection. The dimensions, in particular the horizontal projection, in turn depend on the selected type of facade cladding.

Restricting the material selection of the fire stops to sheet steel is based on the positive effect of such horizontal fire stops in comparison to fire stops made from timber, which was confirmed within long-term tests. Eventually, the timber

fire stops contributed to the horizontal spread of fire due to their combustibility [22]. Despite this, alternative materials could be developed for use as fire stops, yet also require verification in a project-related approval procedure.

The connectors chosen to attach the horizontal fire stop must be fixed to a robust external wall construction element (such as a structural wall plate). The spacing and size of the means of connection must be selected to ensure that thermal stress events do not cause deformations. The basis for these requirements is that fire stops made from sheet steel expand under thermal stress, which may lead to gaps opening between bolted connections applied to the fire stops, which then favour the spread of fire in that area. Therefore, the longitudinal butt joints of the fire stops must be joined mechanically to produce a force-fit connection without a gap (e.g. an overlapping butt joint with a depth of at least 150 mm and at least two connectors on each side) [23].

Internal corners such as those shown in Fig. 13 and 14 a have a notable influence on the flame height and the temperatures resulting from these flames in facade fires [24]. Therefore special precautions (longer projections of the fire stops depending on the type of cladding) must be taken in internal corners of external walls to limit the spread of fire. The same applies to the area surrounding fire walls. The technical building rules provide various options for achieving this in practice [25].

Accessibility and effective firefighting

Each side of the building with an external wall cladding made from timber or wood-based materials must allow effective firefighting. However, this does not necessarily mean either dedicated access, drive-through vehicle routes,

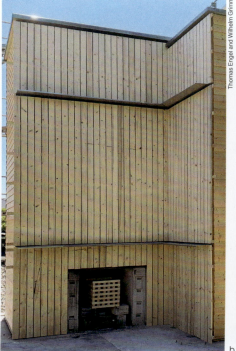

13a   b

22

or stable surfaces for installation of fire-fighting equipment in accordance with the German guidelines for areas for fire brigade use [26]. It is more about ensuring the basic accessibility to the affected building sides.

Whether effective firefighting actions are possible depends not only on the building height but also on the accessibility of the facade, for example by means of balconies, external walkways, windows, flat roofs or fire brigade aerial rescue equipment. A set of specialist recommendations for effective firefighting on wooden facades provides advice on this issue [27]. Ultimately, effective firefighting arrangements are always likely to result from close cooperation with the relevant local fire department.

Notes

[1] Werther, Norman et al.: Hintergründe und Nach-weisgrundlagen zur Brandschutzbemessung von Brettsperrholzkonstruktionen – Teil 1 In: Bautechnik 99, issue 8/2022, pp. 587–593. https://doi.org/10.1002/bate.202200041
[2] DIN EN 1995-1-2:2010-12 Eurocode 5: Design of timber structures – Part 1–2: General – Structural fire design
[3] As note 1
[4] Muster-Richtlinie über brandschutztechnische Anforderungen an hochfeuerhemmende Bauteile in Holzbauweise – M-HFHHolzR. Version July 2004
[5] Muster-Richtlinie über brandschutztechnische Anforderungen an Bauteile und Außenwand-bekleidungen in Holzbauweise (MHolzBauRL). Version October 2020. Edition 4, 21.06.2021
[6] Engel, Thomas et al.: Schlussbericht zum Ver-bundvorhaben TIMpuls – Brandschutztechnische Grundlagenuntersuchung zur Fortschreibung bauaufsichtlicher Regelungen im Hinblick auf eine erweiterte Anwendung des Holzbaus. Gülzow-Prüzen 2022. https://doi.org/10.14459/2022md1661419
[7] Entwurf Muster-Richtlinie über brandschutz-technische Anforderungen an Bauteile und Außenwandbekleidungen in Holzbauweise (MHolzBauRL). Version 18 September 2023
[8] ibid.
[9] Molodovsky, Paul; Famers, Gabriele; Waldmann, Timm: Kommentar – Bayerische Bauordnung, 3. Begriffe zu Art. 26 Außenwände; 148. Aktuali-sierung. Munich/Heidelberg 2023
[10] Kehl, Daniel; Weber, Heinz; Hauswirth, Severin: Ist die Hinterlüftung von Holzfassaden ein Muss? In: Bauphysik 32, 3/2010, pp. 144–148. https://doi.org/10.1002/bapi.201010017
[11] DIN 68800-2:2022-02 Holzschutz – Teil 2: Vorbeugende bauliche Maßnahmen im Hochbau
[12] Engel, Thomas: Brandschutz für biogene Fassaden. Dissertation, TU Munich 2023 https://mediatum.ub.tum.de/?id=1715368 Engel, Thomas, Werther, Norman, Structural Means for Fire-Safe Wooden Façade Design. Fire Technology 59, pp 117–151 (2023). https://doi.org/10.1007/s10694-021-01174-2
[13] ibid.
[14] ibid.
[15] ibid.
[16] Muster-Richtlinie über brandschutztechnische Anforderungen an Bauteile und Außenwand-bekleidungen in Holzbauweise (MHolzBauRL). Version October 2020
[17] As note 7
[18] As note 12
[19] ibid.
[20] As note 12 and 7
[21] As note 12 and 7
[22] As note 12
[23] As note 7
[24] As note 12
[25] As note 12 and 16
[26] Richtlinien über Flächen für die Feuerwehr, version February 2007
[27] Empfehlungen der Arbeitsgemeinschaft der Lei-terinnen und Leiter der Berufsfeuerwehren und des Deutschen Feuerwehrverbandes. Wirksame Löscharbeiten an Holzfassaden (2023-03). Date: 21.11.2023

a

b

12 Detail of external wall cladding at external corners (horizontal section)
13 Facade fire test with vertical open siding facade and steel sheet fire stops projecting 250 mm
   a Wall before fire test
   b Facade fire on vertical open wooden siding facade with fire stops exposed to fire. The horizontal spread of fire and the limiting of the vertical spread of fire by the steel fire stops can be clearly seen. Also visible is the thermal deformation of the fire stops due to the effects of temperature, which is why adequate attach-ment is required.
14 Fire stop consisting of 250 mm projecting sheet steel, for fire testing purposes
   a In the internal corner with a welded fire stop element
   b Fire stop exposed to fire from below
   c Flames of a facade fire declining due to the fire stop

14 c

Facades in Context

Stefan Krötsch

1 Log construction with wooden shingles, the *Wurf,* a feature similar to a string course above the windows, provides weather protection, Bregenzer-wälderhaus Ambros, holiday home, Bezau (AT)
2 Half-timbered building with slate tile cladding, pedestrian zone in Herborn (DE)

The repair, adaptation, reinterpretation and extension of facades are established parts of building history – whether for architectural or technical reasons. The most well-known are the redesigned facades of prestige buildings such as churches, which always had to be adapted and re-adapted to changing styles of architecture. But the external walls of everyday buildings have also been subject to continual change over the course of history, often to allow technical improvements such as better thermal insulation or weather protection. In Germany [1], for example, since the Middle Ages whole towns have seen the west-facing or all of the facades of their half-timbered buildings given a cladding of slate tiles subsequently or at the time of construction to provide protection against the weather. Some of this cladding has been highly artistic and ornamental, typical to the image of the towns to the same extent as the load-bearing structure of the half-timbered buildings left exposed has been in other settlements (Fig. 2).

The external cladding with wooden shingles and panelling in the interior of farmhouses in the Bregenzerwald in Vorarlberg, Austria's westernmost state, are early examples of energy-efficiency refurbishments of formerly unclad log buildings (Fig. 1). With the industrial manufacture and consequently cheaper availability of iron nails from 1850 onward, most farmhouses became covered in what is perceived today as their characteristic wooden shingle cladding. The shingles worked as weather protection for the load-bearing external walls with the aim of considerably prolonging their lives, and the additional layer of wood, above all when combined with wooden panelling on the inside of the external walls, greatly increased the thermal resistance and airtightness of these buildings. At the

same time, an unmistakable regional language of form developed from this cladding with its construction details originally conditioned by the material's inherent properties. One example of this is the *Wurf,* a canopy-like cantilevering of the shingles that protects windows, doors and the joint above the plinth masonry against moisture while, at the same time, adding architectural and sculptural appeal to the facades.

Load-bearing structure and cladding

In his *Bekleidungstheorie,* Gottfried Semper assumed that the origins of architecture were simple frames (skeletons) with a textile cover. Successive transformative steps led to the development of buildings with walls, ceilings and floors: "It may be that climatic influences and other circumstances suffice to explain this cultural-historical phenomenon […], it is certain that the beginnings of architecture coincide with the beginnings of textiles. The wall is the architectural element that formally represents and makes visible the enclosed space as such, absolutely, and without reference to secondary concepts. [...] Frameworks that serve to hold, secure, or support this spatial enclosure are requirements that have nothing directly to do with space or the division of space. They are foreign to the original architectural idea and were never form-determining elements to start with." [2] The actual formation of space is intrinsically, in its architectural form and its construction-related configuration, completely different from the load-bearing structure of a building. According to the architectural theorist Michael Gnehm, the re-evaluation of "the relationship between architectural core and envelope, between ornament and structure" can be attributed to Semper: "For him, the significance of the enveloping surface is no longer limited to architectural form-finding but is important

above all in the constitution of space. The envelope takes precedence over the structural core and therefore the wall is derived from the textile envelope." [3]

Curtain wall

The "Five Points of Modern Architecture" [4] by Le Corbusier and Pierre Jeanneret are also based on the assumption that defining space is detached from the function of the load-bearing structure. This is certainly the case for the type of facade often known as a curtain wall. This thinking influenced post-war architecture in the whole of Europe, not only

3
4

3 General refurbishment of the Middle School, Buchloe (DE) 2010, Müller Schurr Architekten
4 Prefabricated timber frame wall element facade, modernization of a block of flats on Grünten-straße, Augsburg (DE) 2012, lattkearchitekten
5 Different degrees of prefabrication of timber frame wall elements
   a Low degree of prefabrication: studs attached to the existing wall, clamping felt insulation and facade construction on site
   b Medium degree of prefabrication: studs and outer sheathing are prefabricated elements, insulation blown-in on site
   c High degree of prefabrication: insulated pre-fabricated timber frame wall elements including windows, facade cladding on site
   d Very high degree of prefabrication: timber frame wall elements including windows and facade cladding

with respect to the existing buildings but also regarding legislation, which began to differentiate between load-bearing and space-enclosing elements. Fire protection in particular places funda-mentally different demands on the load-bearing structure and the spatial enclo-sure of buildings. In follow, as the energy requirements building envelopes needed to meet became more important, the more its components came to be consid-ered specifically and separately from the rest of the building structure. Therefore it also became increasingly common to consider not only transparent but also opaque components of the facade as curtain wall elements. Prefabricating the facade elements simultaneously allowed industrial processes to be more easily implemented and driven forward. Various combinations of load-bearing structures and building envelopes became common in the construction and materialization of closed external walls. This applied not only to new buildings but also, of course, to the extension of existing structures and with respect to the external walls, not least in the case of energy-efficiency modernizations.

Energy-efficiency modernizations

Since the energy crisis in the 1970s, energy-efficiency modernizations of external walls constitute a relevant con-struction measure. Due to the continually increasing requirements for reducing the consumption of heating energy, for greater comfort and more hygienic living conditions, external wall insulation meas-ures have become commonplace. In order to meet national climate goals and the projected efficiency increases called for in the EU EPBD Directive 2023, 2 % of the existing stock in Germany must undergo energy-efficiency modernizations every year (see "Importance of building in existing stock", p. 7ff).

Biogenic building materials

For the energy-efficient modernization of external walls, aside from the most frequently used plastic or mineral based thermal insulation composite systems (ETICS) or mineral fibre insulated and rear-ventilated construction types, those comprising timber and biogenic build-ing materials also find use. Due to its very low thermal conductivity and high strength, wood is particularly suitable for load-bearing structures embedded in the insulation layer for mounting of back-ventilated external wall cladding. In addition, despite their very low ther-mal conductivity, wood and biogenic insulation materials have a considerably higher thermal storage capacity than fossil-based insulation materials or min-eral fibre insulation. For this purpose, typically timber studs are connected to the existing facade. The cavities are filled with insulation. Either wood or mineral fibre based clamping felt is placed between studs and covered with a diffusion open membrane, or studs are covered with panel sheathing and cavities are filled with blown-in cellulose. In both cases, the construction can be concealed on the outside with rear-ventilated facade cladding. In contrast to an ETICS, this type of external wall energy-efficiency modernization is eco-logically high-quality, robust in terms of building physics, easy to repair and supports demolition at the end of its service life. Installation takes place in individual layers successively on site. All other common components involved in external wall renovation (windows, external roller blinds etc.) are to a large extent installed independently of the facade insulation. The methods used today have been fully tested in practice and are extensively covered in the codes. The following section (see p. 28ff.) there-fore focuses on a relatively new type of

external wall energy-efficiency moderni-zation that is not only a special type of construction, it also entails above all a completely different design and building process: modernizing a building using prefabricated frame wall construction (Fig. 5).

Modernization with prefabricated elements

By using prefabricated timber frame wall elements, a common practice in contemporary timber construction is applied to energy-efficient moderniza-tions. This practice predominantly employs prefabricated wall and ceiling elements in Europe today. In contrast to the above-described non-prefabricated construction, the number of layers is increased firstly by sheathing (mostly OSB) with stiffening function on the frame interior and a compensation layer (mostly mineral fibre insulation) facing the existing wall.. In addition, the stud framing is somewhat more complex because it also requires sill beams, wall plates, window sill trimmers and door / window lintels in order to form stable, transportable elements into which other components such as win-dows and external roller blinds can be installed (Fig. 1, p. 28). In order to protect the insulation layer, prefabri-cated elements almost always have external sheathing installed on the exte-rior of the stud framing (mostly wood or gypsum fibreboard).
The first project in Germany in which a largely prefabricated timber frame wall element facade was used for an energy-efficiency modernization was the 2010 general refurbishment of the middle school in Buchloe (Fig. 3). The 4000 m² facade of the school build-ing was refurbished during the summer holidays so that the school could continue operations without any distur-bance.

TES research project

The concept became commonly known in Europe through the "TES Energy Facade" research project, which was undertaken from 2008 to 2010 and led by Frank Lattke at the Chair of Timber Construction (Hermann Kaufmann) in cooperation with the Chair of Timber Structures and Building Construction (Stefan Winter), both at TU Munich, and researchers from Norway and Finland. The project studied various possible application types, the potential of a closed, digital process chain (survey, design, prefabrication and installation) as well as the technical requirements and practical constraints of realizing the concept (load-bearing frame, fire, sound and thermal insulation, integration of building services etc.). Several practice-oriented projects in Germany and Finland arose between 2012 and 2016 in the wake of the widely praised research project (Fig. 4). The incentive for the use of prefabricated external wall modernizations were often the specific requirements of the building project (limited timeframe for the measures to be completed while the building continues to operate) or the initiatives of the timber construction contractors, who anticipated efficiency and quality benefits as well as an uninterrupted workflow from prefabrication, similar to what they had experienced with new construction.

Although the concept was successful in practice and demonstrated its reliability (above all with respect to the speed of construction on site, as well as the accuracy of cost estimates and consistently high levels of quality), and although various timber construction firms in Bavaria, Baden-Württemberg and other states in Germany had gained sufficient experience with the specificities of this concept, the prefabricated approach has not yet been widely adopted. However, the degree of prefabrication for new buildings is increasing and a similar effect is anticipated for modernizations. The additional complexity of the layered construction of prefabricated elements will likely be balanced in terms of building costs in future through the improved quality of processing and construction as well as the expected beneficial effects of scale (serial production) (Fig. 5).

Energiesprong

An industrialized refurbishment system for roofs and facades consisting of timber frame wall elements was developed in the Netherlands in 2010 under the name *Energiesprong* (energy leap in English). The prefabricated building services modules used for the refurbishment of terraced housing are integrated into the roof and contain all components, such as heat pumps, hot water storage, PV modules and inverters. Since 2014 several thousand of the country's terraced houses and some apartment blocks have been refurbished, with the result that the cost per refurbishment measure has dramatically dropped due to the economies of scale. There are now pilot projects employing the system in the United Kingdom, France and Germany, where it was first used in 2020 in Hameln. The German Energy Agency (dena) has published a programme to make the *Energiesprong* system compliant with German building regulations.

Modernization and new construction

Since storey-height, self-supporting timber frame wall elements can be created simply, they are suitable for the modernization of skeleton frame structures by connecting them to the slab edges, thereby establishing a spatial enclosure. This type of refurbishment of existing stock is hardly any different from timber hybrid new construction, which features a load-bearing system consisting of reinforced concrete floor slabs and columns with a building envelope consisting of timber frame wall elements with a high degree of thermal insulation.

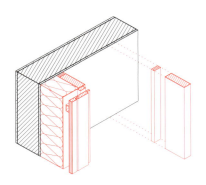

a

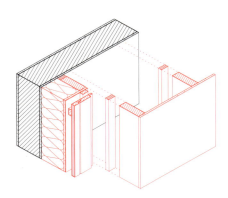

b

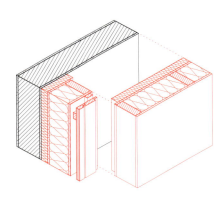

c

Notes
[1] Especially in the Rhenish Slate Mountains and the Sauerland, Siegerland, Bergisches Land, Eifel, Hunsrück and Westerwald regions as well as in the Ore Mountains, in the northern part of Franconia, in the Thüringer Forest and Harz, in Middle and Northern Hesse, in Saxony-Anhalt and in southern Lower Saxony
[2] Semper, Gottfried: Der Stil in den technischen und tektonischen Künsten oder praktische Ästhetik: Ein Handbuch für Techniker, Künstler und Kunstfreunde (vol. 1): Die textile Kunst für sich betrachtet und in Beziehung zur Baukunst; Viertes Hauptstück, Textile Kunst. Das Prinzip der Bekleidung in der Baukunst, §60. Frankfurt a. M. 1860, p. 227f.
[3] Gnehm, Michael: Bekleidungstheorie. In: Arch+, issue 221, pp. 33–39
[4] Le Corbusier; Jeanneret, Pierre: Fünf Punkte zu einer neuen Architektur. In: Die Form. Zeitschrift für gestaltende Arbeit. 2/1927, pp. 272–274

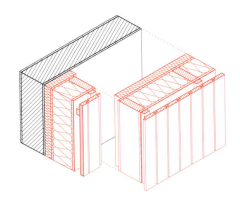

5 d

External Wall Energy-Efficiency Modernizations Using Prefabricated Elements

Stefan Krötsch, Thomas Engel

Prefabricated, highly thermally insulated frame wall elements are an alternative to conventional external wall insulation such as external thermal insulation composite systems (ETICS) or rear-ventilated building envelopes consisting of sheet aluminium or wood. Since these elements can be manufactured mainly from wood and biogenic insulation materials, they are far superior to conventional external wall insulation made of plastic or mineral fibre with respect to their ecological properties. Biogenic insulation layers are more conducive to good building physics, thanks to their thermal inertia and vapour permeability. The crucial advantages, however, arise from the possibility of extensive prefabrication:

- Construction time on site is reduced to a minimum.
- Pollution and disturbance impacting residents, neighbours and the local infrastructure due to building site emissions are minimized.
- Quality, precision and control of construction are optimized by conducting

a digital survey and adopting a systematic planning and production workflow.

- Accurate preliminary planning ensures maximum cost reliability.
- Timber frame wall elements offer plenty of freedom for the facade design.
- The integration of load-bearing construction components supports projecting elements, such as balconies, additional storeys or extensions.
- Building services and active solar components can be easily integrated into the construction.
- Robustness and repairability are ensured by mechanical connections between components.
- Mechanical connections allow easy dismantling of the timber frame wall elements from the existing building, and their components to be separately sorted by material type after the end of the service life.

Frame wall construction can act purely as an insulation layer (e.g. when upgrading existing solid construction walls featur-

ing windows) or as space-enclosing external walls (e.g. when upgrading skeleton frame buildings). They can also be used as extensions enclosing new interior spaces (Fig. 3).
Frame wall elements are commonly layered horizontally and installed one on top of the other, as is similarly the case for new construction. Depending on the options for attachment to the existing building, structural engineering considerations, fire protection concepts or installation conditions, it can also be worthwhile arranging the elements vertically and joining them laterally (Fig. 2).

Construction

Frame wall elements are hybrid constructions consisting of stud framing to which sheathing is attached to provide stiffness. The load-bearing elements and insulation share the same layer. In the case of energy-efficiency modernizations, and depending on the situation,

1   Components of a prefabricated timber frame wall element
2   Possible arrangements for a facade refurbishment
   a Typical horizontal arrangement of frame wall elements, one on top of the other: the elements are transported in their installation orientation.
   b Special case: vertical arrangement of elements for specific reasons, installation more complex as the elements need to be lifted and rotated
3   Principle application, prefabricated facade in relation to the type of load-bearing structure of the existing building:
   a As an insulation layer for windowed facades
   b As an external wall on skeleton frame structures
   c As an external wall on parallel shear wall structures
   d Space-containing elements for balconies, loggias or interior rooms.

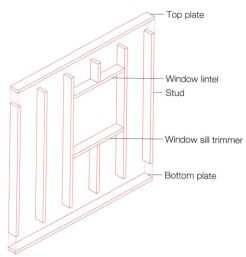
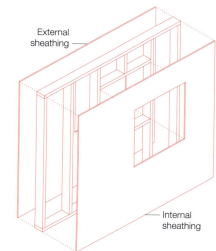

Top plate
Window lintel
Stud
Window sill trimmer
Bottom plate
External sheathing
Internal sheathing

1

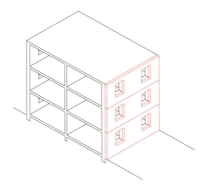

2a

b

the requirements to be satisfied and the geometry of the existing building, it is also possible for the elements to be used as load-bearing building components and thus to create new spaces by converting e.g. balconies into interiors and adding new floor area or balconies.

Stud framing in the case of timber frame wall elements consists mainly of structural timber (KVH) and is made up of wall plates, sill beams, studs, as well as window sills and lintels for the installation of windows (Fig. 1). As interior sheathing with stiffening function, mostly wood based material panels (3-ply panels, OSB) or diagonally arranged boards find use. Vertical loads are distributed through the wall plate into the studs and from there into the bottom plates. The sheathing provides stiffening in the plane of the wall and prevents buckling of the studs in the direction of their weaker axis. The typical spacing of studs is 62.5 cm (on occasions 83.3 cm or other dimensions), so that sheathing can be applied by limiting the amount of wood cuttings. Since compensating for narrow perimeter bays and floor openings isn't difficult to realize, the grid dimensions for stud placement don't impact the architectural design. The dimensioning of the stud frame is typically determined by the necessary insulation thickness rather than structural requirements (e.g. 60/180 to 80/240 mm).

Timber frame wall elements demonstrate high material efficiency for load-bearing purposes. They are also very cost-efficient in their highly thermally insulated type, since cavities are available that can be filled with low-cost insulation material (cellulose flock, wood or mineral fibre based clamping felt), without requiring connectors. The framing avoids causing relevant cold bridges due to the low thermal conductivity of wood. At the same time, load-bearing construction

components permit arranging them in the insulation layer, while load transmission can occur transversely through the insulation layer (connections to balconies, exterior means of access, etc.). The air and vapour barrier of the element coincides with the interior sheathing, allowing prefabricating all airtight connections of further elements (windows, doors, penetrations for building services etc.) under ideal conditions in the workshop. Potential sources of defects for the highly complex external wall components, for example the weather, material shortages, damage and similar events on site can be largely avoided. The external sheathing of the stud framing is usually formed from breathable, water-repellent (hydrophobized) wood fibreboards, light weight wood wool panels or, if necessary, gypsum fibreboards (for rear-ventilated facade cladding). In addition to exterior sheathing, a breathable facade membrane may be used as required.

The external cladding of the element can be an ETICS, a compact facade construction with render applied to the

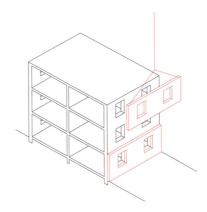

a

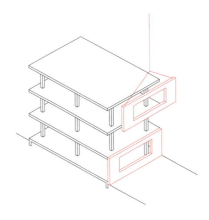

b

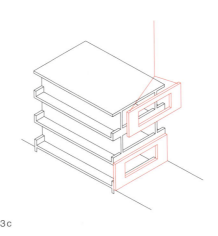

3c

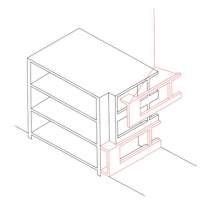

d

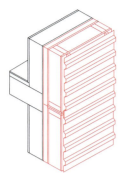 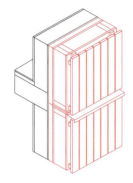 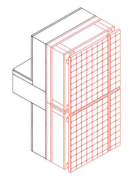 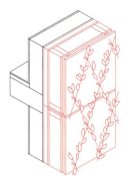

4a   b   c   d

external insulation layer (render substrate panel), or a rear-ventilated facade. In the case of a rear-ventilated construction, all commonly available external wall claddings can be employed, with a few exceptions, depending on architectural requirements. For combustible cladding made from wood or wood-based materials used in buildings of medium height (building class GK 4 and 5 according to German building regulations), the requirements of the German model timber construction guideline must be fulfilled (see "Special aspects of the building regulations", (p. 17ff.)). This typically means that gypsum fibreboard is used for the external sheathing of the timber frame wall elements as a non-combustible layer facing the rear-ventilation cavity. In addition, steel plate fire stops must be installed at each floor level, with the depth of the cantilever projecting beyond the facade cladding being dependent on the type and contour of the facade external surface material (see "Fire barriers", p. 22).

Approval procedures and grand-fathering

In Germany, modernization measures exclusively for external walls can be realized without requiring an application for building permit. In many municipalities, exceeding the property line bordering public space, the building line or boundary, and even the setback line by up to 30 cm is permissible without requiring a permit and as long as the rights of neighbors are respected. For typical multistorey buildings (not high-rise), designers may take into account the provisions of, for example, §61 clause 1 (11) c) and d) of the MBO [1]. This means the replacement of windows and doors along with the openings

provided for them and the attachment of external wall cladding including the measures for thermal insulation, facings and rendering of parts of the building can be considered as exempt from building permit procedures. Generally speaking, a glance at the different rules and regulations shows that this cannot be universally defined for all state building codes. In addition, there are local building regulations such as the design by-laws of the local authorities, which set out the requirements for external wall cladding. Furthermore, an external wall modernization with timber frame wall elements may have implications in areas other than those mentioned above. Therefore, the assumption that no official approval is required should be checked on a case-by-case basis. Fundamentally, all building law regulations must be complied with – irrespective of whether the external wall modernization requires planning approval or a building permit.

Process chain

The opportunities of an extensive digitalized design and prefabrication chain for modern timber new construction can also be applied to the processes of prefabricated external wall modernizations. They contribute to design and construction workflows that function as if tailor-made for building in existing stock. The need for early and detailed information for prefabrication requires involved actors to adopt an approach based on discipline and accuracy for the proposed modernization, which is beneficial for every project involving existing buildings. The process also results in extremely minimized construction time on site, which allows continuous or only very short interruptions to the operation of the building. In addition, the period of disturbance to

the surrounding area (neighbours, local infrastructure) caused by construction work is considerably shortened. On-site waste, dust and noise are practically eliminated by the off-site preassembly of the building components. However, one challenge is that the installation of large but very accurately dimensioned construction elements has to be able to compensate for the sometimes very high dimensional tolerances found in existing structures. Dimensional tolerances can extend beyond specific areas and require a systematic survey of entire facade areas, in follow calling for related compensation measures. This requires not only a very precise dimensional survey but also the systematic inclusion of the existing construction in the design, prefabrication and installation processes in order to precisely align and quickly assemble large-format elements. In this respect, the interface between the existing building and the facade element in modernizations does not differ significantly from the interface between the structural frame or building shell and the timber elements of new construction. In the case of modernizations, the geometry of the existing building is, however, established at an early stage and the size of the tolerances included as a parameter in designing the various layers making up the new facade.

The construction of an external wall modernization using prefabricated elements has a significant effect on the planning and design process. The selection of the construction type should therefore be made at the earliest possible planning stage, preferably in the preliminary design phase (LPH 2), but no later than the design of construction before building permission (LPH 3 in accordance with the German Scales of Fees for Services of Architects and Engineers (HOAI)).

4 Different types of rear-ventilated cladding of
   timber frame wall elements:
   a Non-combustible cladding and framing
   b Biogenic, combustible cladding and framing
      (wood) with fire barriers along slab edges
   c PV or solar thermal panels with and without
      rear-ventilation cavity
   d Green facade with rear-ventilated facade clad-
      ding (e.g. fibre-cement boards)
5 The dimensions of existing buildings can be
   quickly and digitally captured with a photogrammetry app.
6 Digital geometric survey: in addition to the visible
   building geometry, all the relevant information
   about the building geometry must be captured
   and related to the facade geometry: dimensions
   of structural openings, floor elevation, underside
   of ceiling, clear height etc.

5

Survey of the existing building

Most record drawings of existing buildings are not accurate enough or may
deviate greatly from the built situation.
The assessment and a precise geometric
survey of the existing structure play a
key role in prefabricated external wall
modernizations (Fig. 6). Here the decisive factor is less the specific survey
technique but rather the expertise of
the person who performs the survey.
The surveyor must be able to anticipate
the specificities of the fabrication and
installation. The most geometrically accurate survey is useless if the condition
of the surveyed elements is unclear.
The geometric survey and assessment
of the existing building should therefore
go hand in hand. The following must be
ascertained:
• The geometry of the visible parts of the
  existing building, including structural
  frame or shell if present, e.g. dimensions of the facade surfaces, facade
  openings
• Irregularities and deviations from the
  building line, including unevenness
  between facade surfaces
• Identification of the building components
  intended for demolition (e.g. wall cladding, reveal cladding, insulation layers)
• Non-visible but determinant geometry,
  e.g. position of the floors/ceilings on
  the upper storeys, internal wall, room
  heights, window sill heights etc.
• Potential connection points (e.g. position of the slab edges, condition of the
  external wall)

The building geometry should always be
surveyed digitally to avoid loss of precision and to allow the geometrical information to be read into CAD/CAM software
and form the basis for the design. The
survey is typically conducted by a surveyor
or by the timber construction contractor. If

an independent individual, neither surveyor nor contractor, carries out the survey of the existing building, the individual
must be thoroughly briefed by the design
office about the planned construction process, its requirements and constraints.
If the timber construction contractor performs the survey, it is usually much easier
to avoid uncertainties in the detailed information. In this case for various reasons,
including the tendering and award processes for the project, the survey sometimes takes place too late for its information to be available for the design and
execution planning. There are a number
of methods for completing a digital survey:
• Tacheometry
• Photogrammetry
• 3D laser scan

Tacheometry, as the most common
method, is very suitable for recording
every part of the building geometry. It is
easy to use and allows on-site processing of the data. However, features in the
surface contour, such as unevenness of
the facade cannot be captured in detail.
Photogrammetry is excellent for recording and visualizing dimensional information in detail, however, it is difficult to
display or document the recorded information (Fig. 5).
3D laser scans produce very accurate
and complete models. However, they
are susceptible to irregularities in the
measuring process and create huge,
unmanageable quantities of data.
An optimum result is often obtained by
a combination of different surveying

6

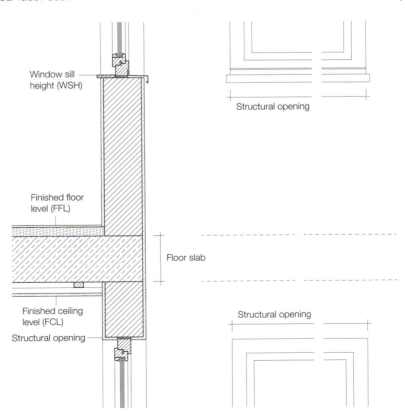

Window sill
height (WSH)

Finished floor
level (FFL)

Floor slab

Finished ceiling
level (FCL)

Structural opening

Structural opening

Structural opening

7 Prefabrication of a timber frame wall element
   a Integrated rotating device in a modular
      gantry system
   b Mobile assembly cell of a modular gantry
      system
   c Sheathing, application of nail connections on
      multi-functional bridge
8 Delivery and lifting with a crane on site
   a Modernization of residential and commercial
      building, Munich (DE) 2016, Braun Krötsch
      Architekten (see Exemplary Projects p. 74ff.)
   b Modernization of block of flats, Augsburg (DE)
      2012, lattkearchitekten

a

b

7 c

methods. For example, tacheometry can be used to survey the most important points on the facade. Then the surface contour can be captured with a 3D laser scan and the point cloud linked with the tacheometric survey data to provide a very good 3D model.

In addition to the geometric survey, the assessment of the building should ascertain all the properties of the existing structure relevant to the design so that sound decisions can be made during the planning phase. The assessment should include for example:

- Determining the load-bearing capacity of existing building components (if necessary through destructive testing or investigation of their physical properties, such as pull-out tests for concrete anchor bolts etc.)
- Establishing foundation soil condition (e.g. soils investigation report)
- Establishing building component condition (e.g. damage, building physics deficiencies)
- Establishing project requirements (e.g. nearby sources of noise)

Planning and design

Ideally the digital geometric survey should lead to the architects and all the specialist engineers producing a well-considered, comprehensive design based on a BIM platform. This 3D model can be transferred in appropriate file formats directly to the workshop planning software of the timber construction contractor. The datasets for the joinery machine, which automatically manufactures the stud framing for the timber frame wall elements, including all the connections, are generated from the workshop planning data. Through this digital process chain from geometric survey to manufacture, inaccuracies, information transfer errors and mismeasurements become more or less impossi-

ble. In parallel, very precise dimensions can be automatically generated at every stage of the design, which results in highly accurate cost management. The necessarily precise planning to prepare for prefabrication also requires many decisions to be made at an earlier stage than in conventional projects. On the one hand, this ensures better organizational planning and discipline, while, on the other hand, the planning expenditure increases in early service phases compared to the German HOAI fee system. Architects, structural engineers as well as design consultants therfore may have to adjust their fees to the actual service provided. This is especially important, if they are not commissioned with execution planning or construction supervision, where the additional work involved in earlier planning phases would be offset by faster and more precise execution.

For the very specific task of external wall modernization with prefabricated timber frame wall elements, it is worthwhile in certain circumstances to consider an alternative contract award procedure (e.g. based on a design and build contract). In that case, the construction contract is awarded at the preliminary design stage. This allows the know-how of the timber construction company to contribute much earlier to the planning of the project, and its way of working and specific capabilities to be taken into consideration. This not only produces synergies and makes planning more efficient; it also prevents errors, misunderstandings and additional costs due to amendments of the detailed drawings after the construction contract has been awarded.

Joinery and prefabrication

Connecting framing and sheathing is conducted in the same way as the prefabrication of components for wall

8a   b

elements in new construction. The only difference is the compensation layer. Attaching it to the existing external wall allows compensating for any surface irregularities. The digital process chain extends from the automated joinery machines to the fabrication of the elements and ensures the highest precision. The installation situation on the existing building sometimes determines the element size to be realized.

The degree of prefabrication can vary greatly and is related to the choices available to the contractor, the assembly options (e.g. site access, site facilities), the layer composition and the connection details. Comparable to new buildings, timber frame wall elements can be extensively prefabricated: insulation, airtight layer, vapour barrier, waterproof layer, windows including all connections, sun protection, facade cladding and siding, window reveals and building services components (e.g. ventilation equipment, electrical installations) can be integrated in the timber workshop (Fig. 7). A high degree of prefabrication minimizes installation time on site and optimizes the quality of construction. However, this requires careful planning and detailing designed with a focus on the assembly process. Lower degrees of prefabrication can perhaps simplify the layer structure or the assembly of the elements. For example, elements not subject to fire safety requirements can be prefabricated as an externally sheathed stud frame with the insulation layer installed on site in the form of blown-in cellulose flock. This latter approach means no compensation layer is required to accommodate the surface irregularities on the existing building. The facade cladding is usually attached on site only if the facade design does not allow access to the fixing points during installation, e.g. if the connectors or the

joints between the elements are not intended to remain visible.

Transport and site logistics

The planning of the transport and site logistics comprises important parameters for determining the dimensions and degree of prefabrication of the timber frame wall elements. In inner-city situations, not only the immediate site surroundings have to be taken into account but also access to the site itself (Fig. 8). The following local circumstances must be considered in the planning of the transport and installation of large elements:

- Site accessibility for the transport of large elements (road alignment/turning radii, unobstructed passage widths/heights, accessibility for vehicles carrying heavy loads etc.)
- Safe storage areas for large elements and reachability by transport vehicles and cranes
- Obstructions within the field of movement of the unloading/installation crane (buildings, trees, street lights/signs, overhead cables etc.)

In order to create suitable conditions for an efficient assembly procedure, it may be necessary in certain circumstances to obtain approvals from the relevant public authorities, e.g. for permission to use public space, taking down street lights/signs, removal of trees and vegetation or paving specific areas.

Adaptation to existing buildings

Prefabricated timber frame wall elements can be manufactured to very precise dimensions. The narrow tolerances of a few millimetres are necessary in order to join large wall elements together using form-fit and force-fit connections. Larger inaccuracies can accumulate over several elements additively and therefore

adversely affect the geometry, the functions of the layers within the cross section and the load transfer. It is therefore necessary to manage the dimensional tolerances of the facade surface to be modernized by incorporating a compensation layer. The timber frame wall element is therefore attached at a distance of a few centimetres in front of the existing facade, which allows the new elements to be installed evenly and independently of any irregularities on the existing facade surface.

The cavity created by this compensation layer is typically filled with non-rigid insulation in order to prevent air convection behind the elements and thus ensure the required insulation performance and fire protection. This is usually done with wood fibre or mineral fibre mats attached to the existing building side of the timber frame wall element. The mats compress or expand on the uneven existing building facade and thus completely fill the cavity. Sometimes, but not often, the compensation layer cavity is filled with blown-in cellulose flock insulation.

In four to eight storeys tall buildings, the compensation layer is completely composed of mineral fibre mats for fire safety reasons to prevent any potential spread of fire in the compensation layer. However, surrounding all openings, a 50 cm wide area must be filled with mineral fibre insulation, which is intended to prevent fire entering the compensation layer (Fig. 18, p. 39).

Element alignment and assembly

An important advantage of extensive prefabrication is quick assembly, which drastically shortens construction time on site. In order to make the most of this potential, precise planning and systematic preparation for the assembly process is required. In practice, two variants in particular have developed, which differ

10

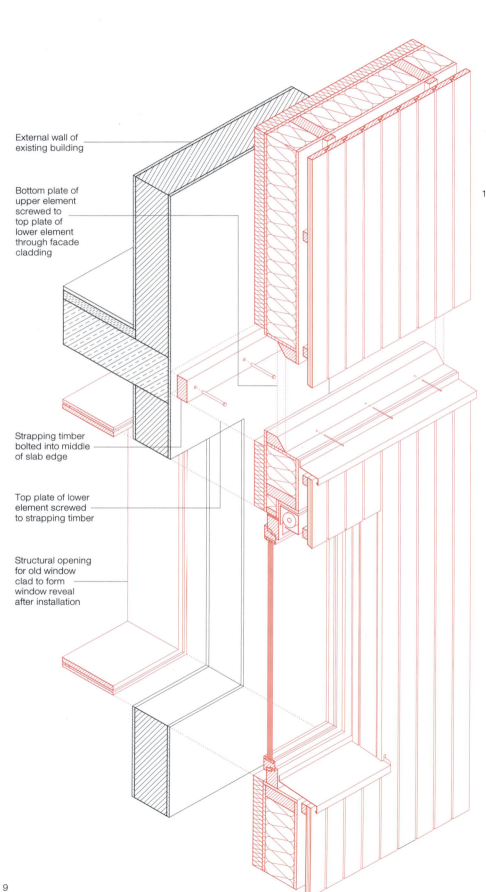

External wall of existing building

Bottom plate of upper element screwed to top plate of lower element through facade cladding

Strapping timber bolted into middle of slab edge

Top plate of lower element screwed to strapping timber

Structural opening for old window clad to form window reveal after installation

9

from one another with respect to the mounting process and the type of support (fastening) along the existing building wall.

Variant 1: Strapping
The unevenness and dimensional tolerances of the existing facade often make it impossible to install the highly precise timber frame wall elements directly onto its surface. In order to assemble elements in a precise manner within an even plane, a means of alignment is necessary to ensure a perfect and rapid installation of what are sometimes very large components. For this purpose, strapping bars can be added in the area of the slab edges. They permit aligning new facade elements and creating load-bearing connections. As preparation for the assembly process, the strapping bars are connected to the external wall intended for modernization (e.g. per aerial platform) and aligned to provide for a plane surface (Fig. 9, 10). Alignment is achieved by inserting individual spacers behind the straps or partially omitting them to compensate for the unevenness of the existing facade. The thickness of the straps matches the thickness of the compensation layer, which is filled with non-rigid insulation. Different variants of this construction type were studied in the TES-EnergyFacade research project (see p. 27) and used in several energy-efficiency modernization projects, for example, the redesign of an apartment complex in Grüntenstraße in Augsburg (Fig. 10).

Variant 2: Steel angles
Another option is to align the bottom row of elements during the course of the assembly at a distance equal to the thickness of the compensation layer in front of the existing building wall, then install the remaining elements successively from bottom to top and fasten them to the

11

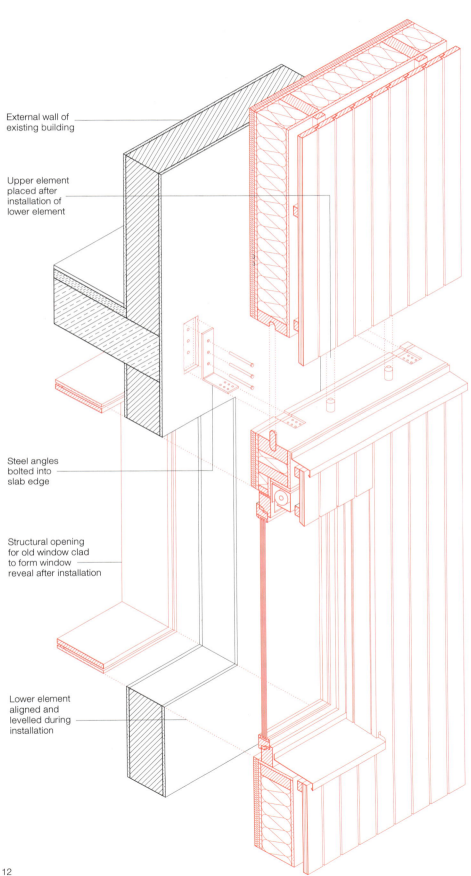

facade with adjustable spacers (usually steel angles) (Fig. 11, 12). The elements can then be installed one on top of the other as part of the installation process in a similar way to new construction, at the correct distance from and geometrically independent of the existing wall. It is also necessary to join the elements one on top of the other using form-fit and force-fit connections, such as by employing beech dowels that allow stacking elements similar to children's building block toys. This construction type has been used in several modernizations, for example, the upgrade of the residential and business building in Donnersbergerstraße in Munich (see p. 74ff.). The modernization of a school in Neuruppin follows a similar principle in which the facade elements are attached storey by storey without framing connected to the load-bearing structure of the existing building (floor slabs or reinforced concrete wall) (see example project, p 82ff.).

Special aspects Variant 1:
- All measurement and alignment works, as well as all bolted connections to the existing facade can be completed in advance and without the time pressure involved in having elements delivered on site beforehand.
- Project-specific unknowns (areas of greater irregularities, pull-out strengths of the substrate into which anchor bolts are drilled etc.) can be clarified in advance.

9 Variant 1: installation of elements on previously aligned and attached strapping, axonometric, scale 1:20
10 Installation of bottom plate / top plate, modernization of an apartment building, Grüntenstraße, Augsburg (DE) 2012, lattkearchitekten
11 Installation of element with steel angles, modernization of residential and commercial building, Munich (DE) 2016, Braun Krötsch Architekten
12 Variant 2: Installation of element using steel angles that are attached during the installation process, axonometric, scale 1:20

External wall of existing building

Upper element placed after installation of lower element

Steel angles bolted into slab edge

Structural opening for old window clad to form window reveal after installation

Lower element aligned and levelled during installation

12

35

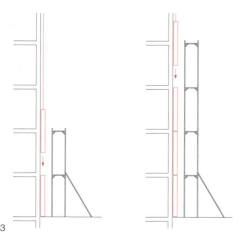

13

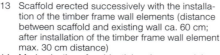

13 Scaffold erected successively with the installa-
    tion of the timber frame wall elements (distance
    between scaffold and existing wall ca. 60 cm;
    after installation of the timber frame wall element
    max. 30 cm distance)
14 Modernization of residential and commercial
    building, Munich (DE) 2016, Braun Krötsch
    Architekten
    a Installation and successive erection of the
       facade scaffold
    b Attachment of a scaffold to the installed elem-
       ents by a left-in-place scaffold bolt (screwed
       into the stud framing)
    c Holes for scaffold bolts placed inconspicuous-
       ly in the shadow below the window sills
15 Installation process depending on the facade
    cladding, horizontal and vertical sections,
    scale 1:20

a

b

14 c

- The storey-by-storey bolted connections between elements and strapping allow assembly to proceed at a rapid pace. No further drilling into existing building walls is required during mounting.
- No steel components are required for attachment to the existing building.
- The compensation layer is relatively thick (ca. 8 cm), because it is defined by the required cross section of the strapping. This results in the airtight layer being relatively closer towards the outside in the sequence of layers in the case of elements with a thin layer of insulation, which may be detrimental to the vapour diffusion performance of the new facade.
- The elements must be attached to the strapping from the outside during installation. Facade cladding installed in the workshop is possible only within limits, e.g. not in the area of attachments to be bolted in place on site.

Special aspects Variant 2:
- There are neither specific procedures for strapping, nor dedicated access scaffolding, nor aerial platforms. The alignment of the new facade surface takes place with the assembly of the lowest horizontal row of elements.
- The compensation layer can be only a few centimetres thick (depending on the evenness of the existing wall surface) and is not defined by the dimensions of the strapping bar. This allows the position of the airtight layer to be optimized in terms of building physics.
- After the alignment of the bottom row, the installation of the elements can proceed rapidly. However, the support angles must be adjusted to accommodate the irregularities in the existing wall during installation of the elements.
- The installation of the steel angle takes place from above on the top plate of the mounted element. This allows the

facade cladding to be installed in the workshop without having to consider the attachment points.
- The elements are very precisely positioned systematically one above the other, for example, by using plug-in connections with beech dowels.
- Situated between the top plate of the lower element and the bottom plate of the upper element, the steel angles are protected from the effects of fire if the top plate and bottom plate are adequately thick and the compensation layer is insulated with mineral fibre in the area of the angle.

The facade scaffold required for installation is typically erected successively in parallel with the mounting of the elements (Fig. 13). The scaffold must be positioned at a sufficient distance from the existing facade (usually 50–60 cm, depending on the thickness of the element) so that the elements can be lifted in between the scaffold and the existing building. After installation of the elements, the distance between scaffold and new exterior should be at least 30 cm in order to prevent the need for fall protection on both scaffold sides. If the scaffold must be fastened to the building, then scaffold anchors (e.g. threaded rods) must have already been installed in the new facade elements in the workshop (Fig. 14). These options for attachment are also very advantageous for future work on the facade (in the course of repair or refurbishment). In addition, they can be architecturally integrated into the appearance of the facade.
Depending on the specific situation, installation can be undertaken without a scaffold but using aerial platforms, if the elements have been extensively prefabricated and no further work is required on the facade after installation (Fig. 15).

Project documentation

In order to make optimum use of the external wall elements over their complete life cycle, it is essential to carefully record at least the following information on all the design documents: the actual component qualities, fasteners, attachment points and building products built or used in the project, including construction-related certificates and other evidential documentation. The life cycle includes all work relating to maintenance, repairs, adjustments and modifications right up to potential demolition and disposal or reuse of the building elements or their components. Since they comprise mechanical fasteners to a major degree, timber frame wall elements are extremely advantageous with respect to repair, reuse and single-material separation in the event of demolition.

Load-bearing structure

The primary function of timber frame wall elements is to act as an insulation layer. In the context of existing buildings, they typically aren't part of the load-bearing structure. The prefabrication and transport of large elements, however, requires them to have sufficient structural capacity to bear loads in excess of their self-weight, in the same way as similar elements in new construction, which are often part of the building's load-bearing structure. The stud framing components (studs, top plate, bottom plate, trimmers, lintels) and the stiffening sheathing combined form a stiff panel capable of carrying vertical and horizontal loads.

Suspended

Typically, the elements are attached at a few support points per element in the area of the floor slab edge and suspended as non-structural facade elements in front of the existing building (Fig. 16a, p. 38).

Facade with render system, horizontal section

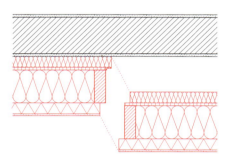

Butt joints; prefabrication including reinforcement layer; application of finishing render and paint on site

Facade with timber siding, horizontal section

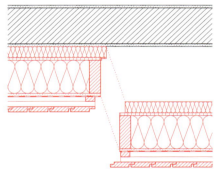

Facade cladding timber sheathing, prefabricated

Panel facade, horizontal section

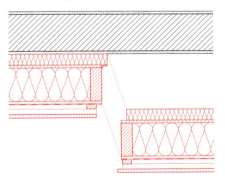

15 Facade panels, prefabricated

Facade with render system, vertical section

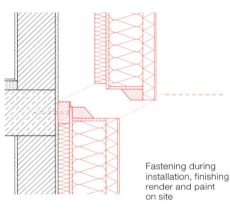

Fastening during installation, finishing render and paint on site

Facade with timber siding, vertical section

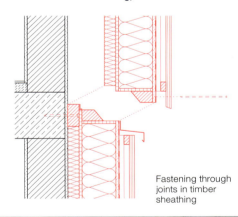

Fastening through joints in timber sheathing

Panel facade, vertical section

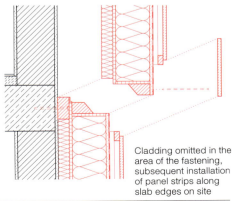

Cladding omitted in the area of the fastening, subsequent installation of panel strips along slab edges on site

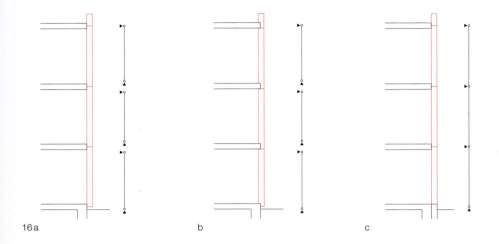

16a   b   c

16 Attachment of facade elements
    a Suspended: elements are fastened to the
       existing building along the floor slab edge
       to transmit vertical and horizontal loads
    b Inserted: elements stand on the floor slab
       edge of the existing building and are fixed to
       the existing building to resist horizontal loads
    c Self-supporting: elements are placed one on
       top of the other on their own foundations in
       front of the existing building, horizontal loads
       transferred through the existing building
17 Balcony, standard detail
    Load transfer within the insulation layer into the
    stud framing of the element for attachment of
    balconies

Damage to the existing building is therefore minimized. Against the background of being able to change the building use and modify component construction at a later date, this can be a great advantage. In this way, for example, temporarily insulated buildings with high-quality existing facades can be largely preserved and returned at a later point in time to their original condition. The timber frame wall elements are generally supported by horizontal strapping or steel angles anchored to the existing facade in the area of the floor slab edges. If the condition of the existing building components is uncertain, the load-bearing capacity of the masonry or concrete can be established by performing pull-out tests at suitable points as part of the design process. The timber frame wall elements are connected by screws or bolts to strapping bars or steel angles respectively during assembly (see "Element alignment and installation", p. 33ff.).

Inserted

In the case of buildings with skeleton frames, the timber frame wall elements may be placed on the floor slab edges instead of being attached in front of the existing building wall (Fig. 16b). Depending on the circumstances, this may considerably simplify the bearing situation, because the elements need only to be secured against horizontal loads. Half of the bottom plate of the timber frame wall elements is set on top of the slab, while the other half cantilevers. For one, this minimizes the bearing surface required for the external wall. Further, this allows covering the slab edges with the insulation layer at least partially. However, the reduced thickness of insulation in this area results in a cold bridge. A gap of a few centimetres at the upper storey floor connection is required in order to be able to manoeuvre the element into

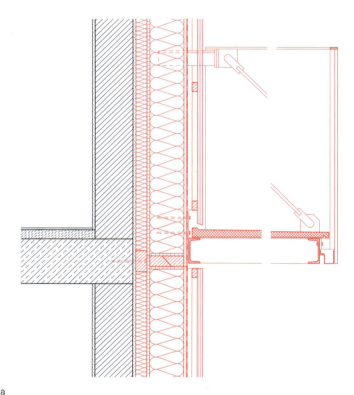

a

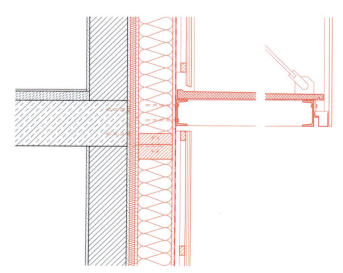

17b

a Variant 1 (strapping): attachment of balcony
  stee beams by screws anchored into studs
  through steel plates
b Variant 2 (steel angles): attachment of balcony
  stee beams by screws anchored directly into
  studs
18 Position and size of the window before (yellow)
  and after (red) the modernization: window and
  solar blind in the insulation layer to maximize
  the clear window opening, plan and section,
  scale 1:20, modernization of residential and
  commercial building, Munich (DE) 2016, Braun
  Krötsch Architekten
  a Plan view
  b Vertical section

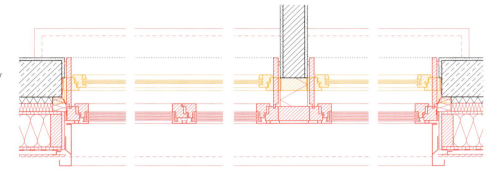

18a

position. This gap must be filled after-
wards in order to prevent noise and fire
from impacting other storeys.

Self-supporting

If the capacity of the load-bearing structure of the existing building is insuffi-
cient to bear the loads of new facade
components, self-supporting timber
frame wall elements can be set on top
of dedicated foundations in front of the
existing building (Fig. 16c). Vertical loads
are distributed from one element to the
next (horizontal elements) or through
the continuous stud framing of the vertical, building-height timber frame wall
elements. In order to transfer horizontal
loads, they feature bolted connections to
the slab edges.

Load-bearing structure in the insulation layer

In contrast to an ETICS or other kinds
of facade insulation attached on site,
the timber frame wall elements allow
attaching other layers or additional components to the stud system with threaded
fasteners. Therefore, not only can all common facade cladding types be attached
without other measures as compact or
rear-ventilated facades but also other
building components such as porches,
fall-protection systems, escape ladders,
lighting etc.
If the timber frame wall elements are
designed to have sufficient load-bearing
capacity, they can also bear the loads
from balconies, walkways or other building components such as extensions
or additional storeys (Fig. 17). This can
be achieved by integrating columns
or beams with larger cross sections or
stronger materials such as glued laminated timber (GLT), beech laminated
veneer lumber (beech LVL) etc. into
the stud frame. If loads are greater,
transverse compressive stress must be
avoided. The same is the case for new

multi-storey timber construction. This can
be achieved by adequately designing
joints between elements (end-grain stud
butt joints, hardwood bottom and top
plates) or by use of full building height
vertical timber frame wall elements with
continuous posts.

Attachment to the existing building

Timber frames typically feature bolted
connections to existing buildings by use
of strapping bars or steel angles along
floor slab edges (see "Element alignment
and assembly", p. 33ff.). On reinforced
concrete external walls, the supports
may be attached in the area of the window parapet to avoid or rectify geometric
problems between supports, window
openings and integrated external sun
protection blinds where present. In the
modernization of the mixed use residential and business building in Munich, this
approach allowed the windows to extend
to the ceiling underside, which increased
the window area and the amount of light
entering deep floor plans, compared to
the situation before the renovation. This
compensated for the loss of daylight that
frequently occurs in energy-efficiency
modernizations due to new triple glazing
and deep window reveals (Fig. 18).

Fire protection

In terms of fire protection, requirements
in place are lower for non-load-bearing
external walls than for their load-bearing
counterparts (Fig. 19, p. 40). In German
building classes 4 and 5 respectively,
load-bearing external walls must guaran-
tee a fire resistance of either 60 (three
to five storeys above ground) or 90 (five
to nine storeys above ground) minutes.
There are no requirements in place for
non-load-bearing external walls consisting of non-combustible building materials.

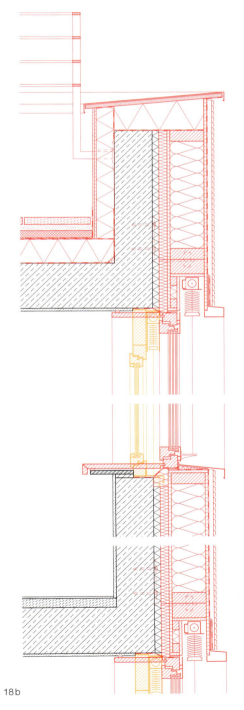

18b

If they consist of combustible materials such as timber, then they must be classified as a wall with a 30-minute fire resistance rating (integrity and thermal insulation) by German building regulations (*raumabschließend feuerhemmend*) (German rating: F 30-B or W 30 [2]; European: from inside to outside E 30 (i→o) and from outside to inside EI 30-ef (i←o) [3]). No requirements relating to their integrity are specified for non-load-bearing external walls for buildings with three or fewer storeys above ground. If timber frame wall elements find use as insulated external walls of existing buildings, they are almost always non-load-bearing (for

exceptions see "Load-bearing structure in the insulation layer", p. 39). The applicable requirements for buildings with more than three storeys above ground can be easily fulfilled with the usual additional construction elements (inner sheathing with wood-based boards or mineral boards, stud framing with cellulose, wood fibre or mineral fibre insulation, outer sheathing with wood-based boards or mineral boards). For this purpose, components either need technical approval or fire test based permits. Or, they need to comply with officially enacted technical building rules. DIN 4102-4, for instance, comprises applica-

ble and verified product-neutral element compositions [4]. The future revision of EN 1995-1-2 (2nd generation) will expand and refine this standard, which is relevant for modern timber construction.
The fire protection goal of the requirements for external walls is the "adequately long" prevention of storey-to-storey fire spread and the spread of fire along the facade (see "Fire protection for timber facades", p. 19ff.). External walls are required to be appropriately robust. This requirement is fulfilled by a construction made of combustible materials, which is classified as a wall with a fire resistance of 30 minutes. The following specific

Building class 1	Building class 2	Building class 3	Building class 4	Building class 5

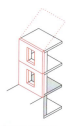 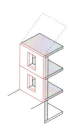  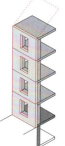 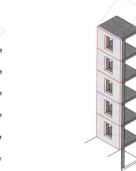

Existing walls

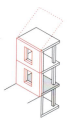   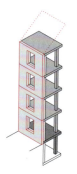 

☐ No requirements
▨ (R)EI 30
▨ (R)EI 60
■ (R)EI 90
— Existing walls
— Refurbishment with timber frame walls

19 Non-load-bearing external wall

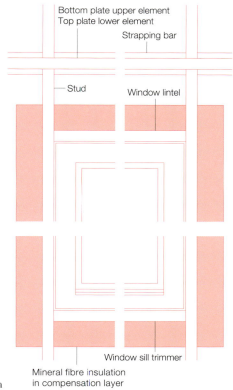

Mineral fibre insulation
in compensation layer

a

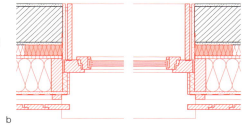

b

requirements arise from this for timber frame wall elements used in external wall modernizations:

- Robust external wall in terms of fire resistance (in the case of constructions made from combustible materials) if external walls providing complete enclosure integrity are absent
- Prevention of fire spread through the compensation layer (between the existing wall and the timber frame wall element)
- Prevention of fire spread through the timber frame wall element itself (mainly through cavity fires in voids in the insulation layer)
- Prevention of fire spread through the facade cladding (above all in the case of combustible, rear-ventilated facade cladding)

If the existing external wall already fulfils the requirement of 30-minute fire resistance, then in theory there is no requirement for the timber frame wall element to provide enclosure integrity. In practical terms, however, the element must fulfil 30-minute fire resistance in order to provide proof of robustness. In this case, the compensation layer between the building and the facade element is problematic. Typically the spread of fire in this layer would be stopped by insulation of the compensation layer consisting of cavity-filling compressed mineral wool. If cellulose insulation is used for insulating the compensation layer, any openings in the area of the existing wall can be filled with a 50-cm-wide strip of mineral wool insulation. Alternatively, or as an additional measure, fire protective cladding (gypsum board type F/gypsum fibre-board) can be fixed over the gap between the existing wall and the facade element (Fig. 20).
If the existing external wall fails to meet the robustness requirement or is simply

absent (e.g. the building to be modernized has a skeleton frame), the timber frame wall fulfils the purpose of enclosure integrity. To avoid cold bridges, new insulation layers are typically suspended in front of the existing construction (floor slabs). In this way, the floor slab does not interrupt the external wall. This is not only the case with external wall energy-efficiency modernizations using timber frame wall elements but also, for example, with glazed post-and-beam facades. To cover this eventuality, building regulations have also changed in the past. The connection of the floor slabs to the external wall must fulfil the following requirements: "Storey floor slabs, as the load-bearing and fire-separating components between storeys in the event of fire, must be structurally stable and resistant to the spread of fire for an adequately long period." Floor slabs must therefore preserve the enclosure integrity up to the external wall, e.g. in the case of glazed post-and-beam facades (facade or external wall with no fire resistance rating). The glass is permitted to be continued past the floor slab edge. The gap between the floor slab edge and the glass must, however, be closed with suitable mineral wool insulation and the room enclosure function ensured. No requirements are stipulated for the external wall, even if it continues in front and past the floor slab edge, except that any combustible materials used there must be rated as 30-minute fire resistance. The legal note to the Bavarian building regulations (BayBO) thus states: "In

19 Fire protection requirements for load-bearing and non-load-bearing external walls in buildings class GK 1 to 5
20 Modernization of block of flats on Grüntenstraße, Augsburg (DE) 2012, lattkearchitekten
  a Mineral fibre insulation to prevent fire in the compensation layer in the area of the window, elevation
  b Horizontal section window reveal, scale 1:20
  c Vertical section window reveal, scale 1:20

20c

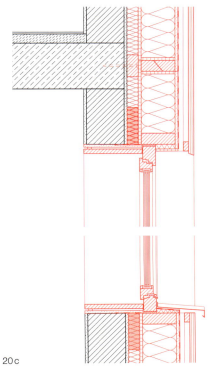

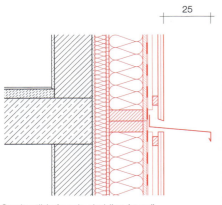

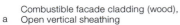

a   Combustible facade cladding (wood),
     Open vertical sheathing

22

b   Combustible facade cladding (wood), horizontal
     tongue and groove joints

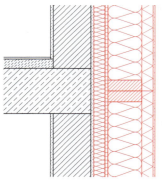

c   Non-combustible facade cladding, render substrate
     panel, low flammability (*schwer entflammbar*), render

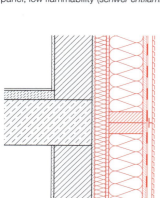

21 d Non-combustible facade cladding, metal, fire stop
      in rear-ventilation cavity every second storey

accordance with clause 3, the connection of the storey floor slabs to the external wall must satisfy the requirements in clause 1 (1). This refers to the enclosure integrity. The regulation takes into account the increasingly common facade systems that pass the slab edges and are not interrupted by them. The remaining construction gap between the floor slab edge and the interior of the facade is considered in principle as an opening and therefore must be closed so that the floor slab also remains resistant to the spread of fire from storey to storey for an adequately long time period. Filling the construction gap with non-combustible building materials that retain their shape in a fire (e.g. concrete, mortar, mineral insulation with a melting point of at least 1000 °C is usually sufficient, […])." [5]. What is being referred to here as well is the connection and the remaining construction gap, but not the external wall as such.

The spread of fire through the timber frame wall elements themselves is typically prevented by the component construction: the insulated cavity within the stud framing is enclosed on the one hand by the sheathing (wood-based boards or mineral boards) and on the other by the studs (vertical borders), bottom plate, top plate (horizontal borders) and by the studs, lintels and trimmers (at window and door openings).

External wall cladding

The external wall cladding and /or the facade have a significant influence on the spread of fire. External timber frame wall elements can be used in combination with compact or rear-ventilated facades and covered with a wide range of different cladding types. Green facades designed to allow planting are also used (Fig. 4 d, p. 30). With respect to fire protection, the construction of the external wall depends in principle on whether the cladding is

made of combustible or non-combustible materials (Fig. 21). Even if the cladding consists of non-combustible materials, special precautions against the spread of fire must be taken in the case of rear-ventilated facades [6]. Moreover, they must satisfy the provisions of the proof of applicability. Requirements (e.g. rendered exterior) apply to, among other things, the enclosure integrity of combustible timber frame wall elements of the external wall in the area of the rear-ventilation cavity. Similar regulations apply to rear-ventilated facades made from low flammability (*schwer entflammbar*) cladding as long as the facade system also incorporates building materials classified as hardly flammable. This information is also contained in the respective verification of fitness for application.

However, cladding consisting of combustible building materials such as wood is also permitted. What has to be considered in this respect for buildings with more than three storeys above ground is described in the section on "Fire protection for timber facades" (p. 19ff.).

Building physics

Thermal insulation, noise control and moisture protection are the most important considerations in building physics engineering. Such measures are optimally provided by a largely continuous sequence of layers forming the building envelope and a similar largely continuous separation of functional units (floors and ceilings).

Sound insulation

By adding further component layers and providing a reliable degree of airtightness, the refurbishment of the building envelope, as a rule, clearly improves protection from external noise.

21 Fire stops for different facade cladding in building classes with more than three storeys above ground, scale 1:20
   a Open, vertical timber sheathing: steel sheet fire stop at the level of every slab edge, projection 25 cm
   b Closed, interlocked, vertical timber sheathing: steel sheet fire stop at the level of every slab edge, projection 5 cm
   c Compact, rendered facade: no fire stops required
   d Rear-ventilated, non-combustible facade cladding: interruption in the rear-ventilation cavity every second storey
22 Fire stop
23 Relatively homogeneous isothermal curve by installing the window in the insulation layer
24 Interior sheathing: the timber frame wall element is the airtight layer for the building envelope. Additional airtight joints between windows and the existing building prevent noise and smoke transfer between storeys through the compensation layer.

New windows, which today are often triple-glazed and can be closed much more tightly than their predecessors, noticeably increase sound insulation against outdoor noise. Although these measures are designed to provide higher objective levels of comfort for building users, it sometimes isn't perceived that way. With the reduced impact of external sources of noise, sound transmitted between rooms or functional units within the building is now perceived as louder than it ever was before, causing sound protection inside the building occasionally to become subjectively worse. Building users should be advised in advance about this effect to avoid later dissatisfaction.

Thermal insulation

The primary goal of an energy-efficiency modernization is to reduce the energy demand of the building, depending on the overall concept and thickness of insulation, to the level of a zero-energy or passive house. Prefabricated timber frame wall elements are a reliable and proven means of achieving this goal. Prefabrication allows the project to be thoroughly planned down to the last detail and ensures optimum conditions for installation by the very precise and controlled manufacture of the complex connections of the external wall components. It can therefore be assumed that prefabricated facade elements are considerably more effective in terms of airtightness, component connections and lack of cold bridges than external wall insulation structures completely built on site. The windows installed in the timber frame wall elements are already integrated in the insulation layer during prefabrication. Cold bridges related to component geometry are avoided (Fig. 23).

The inside (i.e. facing the existing building) sheathing of the timber frame element

ents (e.g. OSB) usually form the airtight layer. Joints between elements need to be planned to avoid gaps in the airtight layer. Since this layer connects directly to the existing building wall and, as a rule, is no longer accessible after installation, this connection detail needs to be designed with great care. To prevent any condensation from occurring inside the component, the insulation within the compensation layer and covered by the airtight layer must contribute no more than 25 % of the total insulation effect. If the existing masonry already has relatively low thermal conductivity (constructed after ca. 1980), then the possibility of condensation should be investigated at the design stage.

Windows should be connected to the airtight layer of the timber frame wall element. In addition, an airtight connection to the interior render of the existing building should be created in the area of the windows to prevent potential transmission of sound and smoke gas through the compensation layer into other storeys or functional units (Fig. 24).

The insulation considerably improves the thermal comfort inside the building by noticeably increasing the temperature of the indoor surfaces of the external walls in winter and, in an ideal case (with U-values of 0.15 W/m²K or better), brings them to temperatures similar to those of the surfaces of internal walls so that there is no perceivable indoor radiant asymmetry. An airtight building envelope and airtight windows also prevent unpleasant draught. Much lower flow temperatures are thus required, which not only saves energy overall but also allows modern heating systems such as heat pumps with their extremely high efficiencies to be used, even if the existing heat distribution (heat pipe system) and heat transfer elements (radiators) remain.

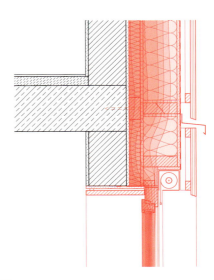

23

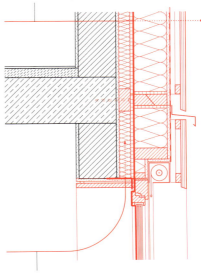

Air and vapour tightness of the building envelope

Airtightness between storeys (smoke and sound protection)

24

25

25 Prefabricated building services shaft with sheathing on one side, "Kölner Holzhaus", Architekturbüro Laur
26 Prefabricated building services shaft: vertical facade element with prefabricated risers and downpipes; horizontal distribution in the compensation layer; register and subdistribution in wall niche, isometric
27 Timber frame wall element with integrated ventilation equipment, elevation and section
28 Prefabricated building services shaft, horizontal section, scale 1:20
29 Heating radiator installation flow/return pipes in compensation layer, vertical section, scale 1:20

Building services

Since an energy-efficiency modernization often involves not only the renewal or renovation of the building envelope but also of the building services equipment, it is the ideal opportunity to utilize the greatest possible number of synergy effects for both partial measures. On the one hand, a well-insulated building envelope benefits heating systems that work with lower flow temperatures (e.g. heat pumps, infrared heating). On the other hand, existing buildings that are primarily to receive an energy-efficiency modernization (buildings erected during the post-war period) now require extensive renovation of their building services equipment.

Integrated pipes, ducts and cables
Pipes, ducts and cables for electricity, data, ventilation, heating, water or wastewater are typically installed inside buildings. As a rule, this is the most expedient approach because it allows them to be easily repaired, retrofit or renewed. However, it is sometimes worthwhile placing services in the insulation layer of external wall energy-efficiency modernizations, e.g. if the building is to be modernized while still occupied or being used, and the impact on the users is to be minimized (Fig. 28, 29). In this way, demolition work and loss of usable area can be avoided by employing facing shell structures. Pipes, ducts and cables required for electricity, data, water or heating, can be installed in the compensation layer between the strapping bars. This allows using the available cavity, while the airtight layer (inner sheathing of the timber frame wall element) can remain without penetration, comparable to the installation layer of new construction. The services are installed in this case on site before the elements are attached. Variant 1 is

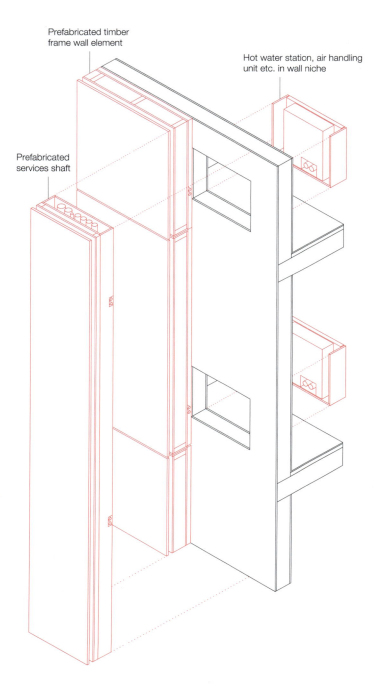

Prefabricated timber frame wall element

Hot water station, air handling unit etc. in wall niche

Prefabricated services shaft

26

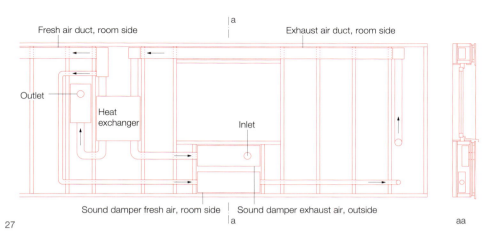

Fresh air duct, room side

Exhaust air duct, room side

Outlet

Heat exchanger

Inlet

Sound damper fresh air, room side | Sound damper exhaust air, outside

27

aa

suitable for this purpose. Elements are connected to a strapping bar (see p. 34f.). The cavity defined thus offers improved protection for service lines during assembly (Fig. 29).

However, building services equipment or pipes etc. may also be installed inside the timber frame wall elements. This is primarily advantageous for large ducts or pipes (for ventilation or roof drainage etc.) or for connections to building services equipment that would have to penetrate the building envelope anyway (stand-alone ventilation units, electrical installations for solar protection, photovoltaics and other outdoor equipment). Larger components, such as heat exchangers and sound dampers for ventilation equipment, can also be integrated where the energy concept permits the resulting weak point in the insulation layer. Individually controlled room fans that are not part of the centrally controlled ventilation system can be fitted in the area of the window reveals so that no additional openings need to be made in the existing external wall (Fig. 27).

Penetrations

If ventilation ducts or other services require penetrations in other areas, then the openings in the existing wall should be created prior to the installation of the timber frame wall elements. This prevents subsequent damage to the airtight layer, and debris from the demolition work in the wall does not accidentally fall into the compensation layer cavity. The position of the services opening in the existing wall must coincide exactly with its counterpart in the prefabricated timber frame wall element. Similar to installing windows, the penetrations for service lines in the insulation layer require sealing them off in order to prevent increased noise transmission between functional units or the spread of fire or smoke through the insulation layer.. A suitable bulkhead can usually be fitted in the area of the penetration through the existing wall. If building services components are integrated into the timber frame wall element, then the affected cavity areas are to be lined with fire protective cladding if necessary.

Inspection openings

Inspection openings may be required for specific areas if pipes, ducts, cables etc. are placed in the insulation layer (compensation layer or element) (Fig. 28, 29). Access from the outside requires that joints between the openings and the walls are watertight, windproof and, if necessary, airtight (when installing services through the compensation layer) in order to ensure effective thermal insulation and moisture protection. For these reasons, the opening receives a circumferential rubber seal. A drive-in nut is fitted in the factory to eliminate wear on the fastening by repeated opening and closing. In external walls with timber facades on buildings with more than three storeys above ground, the continuity of the noncombustible layer behind the facade cladding must be ensured.

Prefabricated services shafts

A number of different services installations can be grouped together in prefabricated spatial modules as part of an external wall modernization. These modules can be

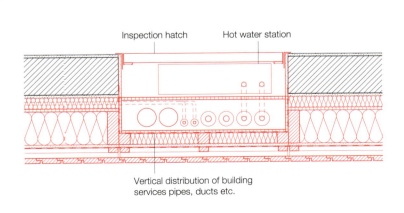

Inspection hatch   Hot water station

Vertical distribution of building services pipes, ducts etc.

28

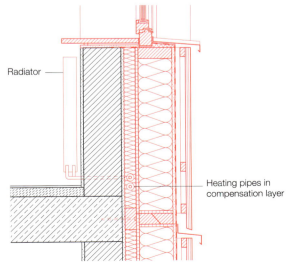

Radiator

Heating pipes in compensation layer

29

Notes
[1] Model Building Regulations (MBO), version November 2002, last amended by resolution of the German Building Ministers Conference dated 22/23.09.2022
[2] Note: F 30 in accordance with DIN 4102-2 and W 30 (external fire exposure curve) in accordance with DIN 4102-3
[3] Note: ef = if the performance is determined using the external fire exposure curve instead of the standard temperature time curve; i ↔ o = in – out, direction of the classified fire resistance period
[4] DIN EN 1995-1-2:2010-12 Eurocode 5: Design of timber structures – Part 1-2: General – Structural fire design
[5] Molodovsky, Paul; Famers, Gabriele; Waldmann, Timm: Kommentar – Bayerische Bauordnung, 9.1 Anschluss der Decke an die Außenwand (Abs. 3) zu Art. 29 Decken, 148th update. Munich/Heidelberg 2023
[6] Appendix 6 Muster-Verwaltungsvorschrift Technische Baubestimmungen 2023/1 – MVV TB 2023/1 – with typographical error correction dated 10 May 2023

attached in front of the existing wall in a similar way to the timber frame wall elements themselves but as part of the insulation layer (Fig. 25, 26, p. 44). Such measures allow combining heat registers, heat exchangers, sound dampeners for ventilation systems and different types of risers. In this way, it is possible to arrange for access from inside or outside the building through inspection panels. Thus the building services equipment can be to a large extent preinstalled under optimal workshop conditions so that construction time on site is significantly shortened and less work is required to be carried out inside the building. The pipes etc. in the prefabricated shaft need only to be connected to the respective services networks on site.

Photovoltaic and solar thermal systems

Timber frame wall elements can also be fitted with photovoltaic or solar thermal panels instead of conventional facade cladding (Fig. 30). Both element types can be fitted flush with ordinary facade cladding by appropriately adjusting the framing. Cabling for the photovoltaics can be fed through the rear-ventilation cavity of the facade and bundled to lead them into the building. The pipework for

solar thermal collectors can be taken directly through the timber frame wall elements during prefabrication and connected to the pipes in the compensation layer or inside the building during installation of the elements. Rear ventilation, which these facades typically offer, is advantageous for photovoltaic panels, because the efficiency of the panels is increased by cooling along their backside. On the other hand, it reduces the output from solar thermal collectors. In the latter case, the rear ventilation should be blocked off. In addition, all building materials installed behind the collector should be generally suitable for high temperatures (e.g. the facade membrane).

Integrated solar protection

As a rule, any required sun protection blinds can be simply integrated into the new external wall construction, especially with rear-ventilated facades. This ensures that the sun protection blinds are not only safe from mechanical damage and the weather but also that they are optimally integrated into the architecture. This can be conducted in a relatively simple manner if existing buildings feature window lintels, which allows geometrically disentangling the means of connection of

elements in the area of the floor slab, for instance when installing a window or sun protection. Special structural measures or fastenings in the window parapet area of the storey above may be required for the installation of room-height windows (see "Attachment to the existing building", p. 39). If blinds are to be integrated into a facade as part of the modernization of a building with a skeleton frame, then a false lintel or an alternative sun protection system such as sliding shutters are required (Fig. 32).

30 Active solar facade cladding
a Solar thermal panel: rear ventilation blocked to improve output
b Photovoltaic panel: rear ventilation for cooling and increasing output
31 Photovoltaics integrated into a building, Aktiv-Stadthaus, Frankfurt (DE) 2015, HHS Planer + Architekten
32 Various construction types for window installation depending on the type of sun protection and external wall modernization construction system (Variant 1: strapping, see Fig. 9, p. 34 or Variant 2: steel angles, see Fig. 12, p. 35)

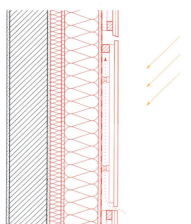
b

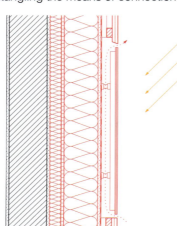

31

Jakob Schoof

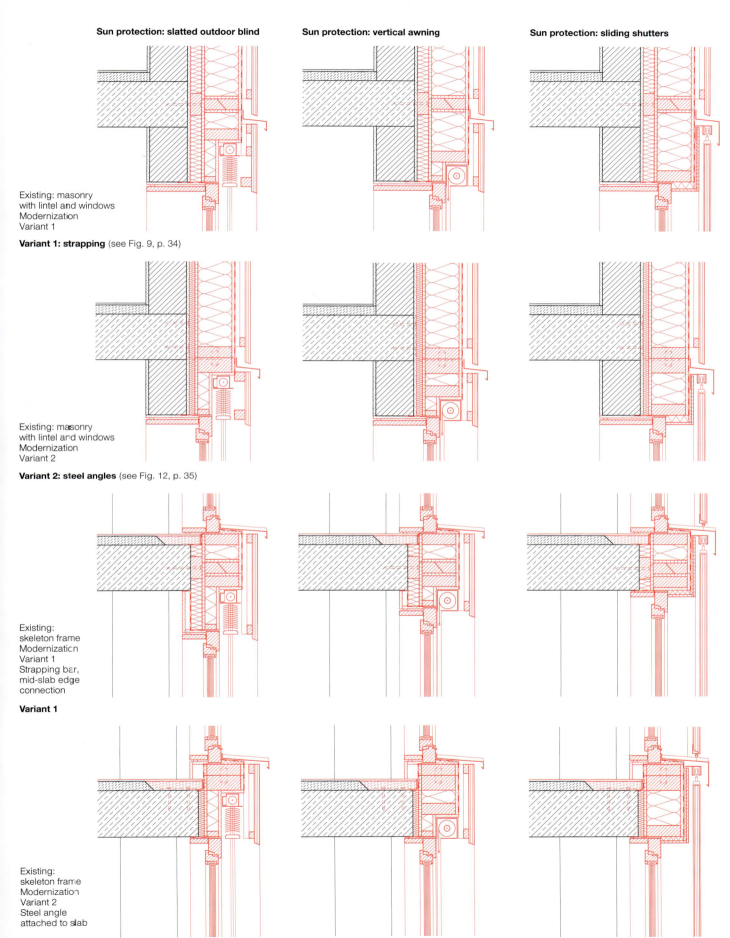

Sun protection: slatted outdoor blind **Sun protection: vertical awning** **Sun protection: sliding shutters**

Existing: masonry
with lintel and windows
Modernization
Variant 1

Variant 1: strapping (see Fig. 9, p. 34)

Existing: masonry
with lintel and windows
Modernization
Variant 2

Variant 2: steel angles (see Fig. 12, p. 35)

Existing:
skeleton frame
Modernization
Variant 1
Strapping bar,
mid-slab edge
connection

Variant 1

Existing:
skeleton frame
Modernization
Variant 2
Steel angle
attached to slab

32 **Variant 2**

The Potential of Vertical Extensions –
Building Without Consuming Land

Manfred Stieglmeier

1 Extending vertically to conserve resources

Adding storeys and extending buildings requires considering the social context. There is a broad consensus today that the available resources are finite. In the light of this fact, the sustainable use of raw materials and energy is gaining in importance. The idea plays a key role particularly in the built environment. The construction sector is responsible for a large proportion of our CO_2 emissions (see "The Social Challenges of Building", p. 7ff.). In Europe, the figure is 38% [1], representing a considerable contribution to global warming. The alternative to demolition and new construction is urban densification through adding storeys and extensions. The preservation and expansion of the existing building fabric stands in stark contrast to what would otherwise be the case: demolition, disposal and building anew. The involved consumption of resources and primary energy and resulting CO_2 emissions would be far higher.

Existing structures are a valuable resource store and contain a considerable amount of embodied energy, which is held in the materials and structures resulting from the manufacture, transport and erection of the building. Concepts for the use and preservation of embodied energy and for the reduction of emissions are required in order to ensure resources are used sustainably. The energy-efficiency refurbishment of the existing stock and the continued use of already built structures will achieve savings of material-related emissions compared to new construction (see "Life Cycle Assessment in Timber Construction and Existing Stock", p. 12ff). Up to 80% of the buildings existing today will still be here in 2050 [2] and will therefore form the basis of the building fabric for the buildings of the future.

One of the most challenging tasks for societies is to create adequate living space without adversely affecting the natural terrain through excessive soil sealing. In this context, adding storeys and extensions to existing buildings represents an essential and effective approach to finding a solution. The vertical extension of existing structures not only creates additional housing by making more efficient use of available built-up area but also does not contribute to the sealing of ground surfaces (Fig. 1). From the point of view of resource conservation, this allows three important points to be made on the benefits of extending vertically:

· Reduction of the consumption of land
· Improvement of the energy assessment in combination with an energy-efficiency refurbishment
· Extended service life of existing structures

Densification strategies

Adding storeys in the form of roof extensions and therefore reusing the existing building fabric can be seen as an alternative to new construction and opens new possibilities for balancing the challenges of satisfying the growing demand for housing while retaining natural ground surfaces. In addition, purposeful strategies for urban development and densification are required. The Deutschlandstudie 2019 study [3] by TU Darmstadt and the Eduard Pestel Institut für Systemforschung e.V. investigated the potential of vertical extensions in the urban context of German cities, municipalities and smaller local authorities to generate new living space. Compared to the Deutschlandstudie 2016 [4], which mainly examined adding storeys to multi-family dwellings, the focus of the new study extended to the additional potential of non-residential buildings in city centres for creating new housing. Looking beyond the potential of vertical extensions to buildings, the study examined the possibility of creating further residential space by changing the use

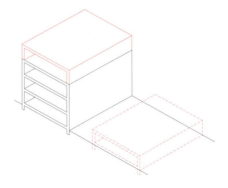

a   Reduction of land consumption

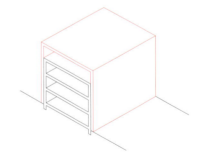

b   Improvement of the energy assessment in combination with an energy-efficiency modernization

1 c   Extended service life of existing structures

Stijn Nagels

Volker Wortmeyer

2

of empty office and administration buildings in the region. This analysis also took into account the existing need for housing and the excess supply of unused office space. The total potential was estimated at between 2.3 and 2.7 million housing units while only 1.1 to 1.5 million would be realizable by adding storeys to residential buildings. The further ca. 1.3 million homes could be generated by the densification of office and administration buildings, single-storey retail facilities and parking garages. The reduction of energy consumption by extending non-residential buildings vertically is estimated to be up to 50 % due to the reduction of cooling loads in summer. For extensions with construction types that adhere to low energy standards,

additional energy demands are low also due to the fact that the existing building services can be used.

Housing complex in Salzburg
The example of the housing complex on Friedrich-Inhauser-Straße in Salzburg makes the connection clear. In terms of building technology, the three blocks of flats with a total of 75 units from 1985 were showing their age. In addition to their inadequate energy efficiency, they failed to meet modern construction standards such as barrier-free accessibility and adequate lighting of the rooms. As part of a research project at Salzburg University of Applied Sciences (FH Salzburg) which worked on establishing an overall energy concept, the owner decided to renovate

the structures instead of demolishing and replacing them with new buidings. The timber hybrid two-storey roof extensions, which generated an additional 24 subsidized housing units, were part of economic considerations in the realization of an energy-efficiency concept (Fig. 2).
The shallow building depth was suitable for a roof extension with solid timber loadbearing walls. The floor slabs consist of reinforced concrete, due to the applied building class (GK) 5 and the requirements issued by building authorities. The gable walls, which characterized the appearance of the building complex, were to be retained. This formed part of the response from the cs-architektur design team to the requirements of the

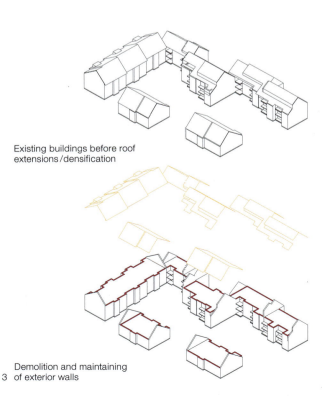

Existing buildings before roof
extensions / densification

3 Demolition and maintaining
of exterior walls

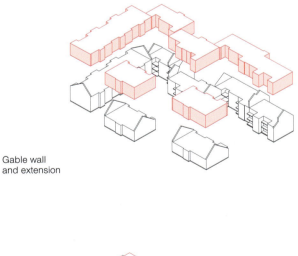

cs-architektur

Gable wall
and extension

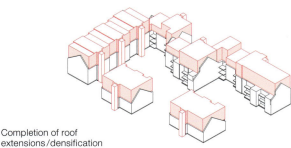

Completion of roof
extensions / densification

50

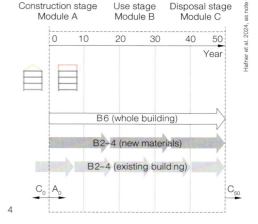

2 Two-storey roof extension, timber hybrid construction, housing complex Friedrich-Inhauser-Straße, Salzburg (AT) 2021, cs-architektur
3 Transformation process of adding two storeys to the existing housing complex Friedrich-Inhauser-Straße, Salzburg (AT) 2021, cs-architektur
4 Application of life cycle modules to roof extension projects
5 Emissions over the life cycle of a building with added storeys compared to fictitious demolition/new construction based on a life cycle analysis method adjusted for additional storeys comparable to Fig. 4 [6]. C0 + A0 is the energy balance at time 0. This includes all the components that were removed (e.g. roof construction, windows) from the existing building and all new materials delivered on site (e.g. roof, insulation, windows).

architectural and urban planning committee of the city of Salzburg. The functional program includes shared terraces to facilitate easy communication between the residents, a bicycle garage and a mobility point.
The design was awarded the Klimaaktiv-Standard Gold. Its construction is defined by the material timber and the energy concept uses wastewater to generate heat in addition to an exhaust air heat pump.

Ecological aspects

From an ecological point of view, several advantages arise from adding storeys and extensions to an existing building. Generally beneficial in energy-related terms is redensification based on the notion of inward urban growth as opposed to municipalities assigning land for new construction along the urban fringe. Shortening infrastructural routes and avoiding the increasing consumption of land for residential and commercial development along the urban fringe or in rural areas leads to saving energy and reducing emissions caused by mobility and supplying energy to buildings.
A further advantage of adding storeys to the existing context is, as a rule, the improved energy balance of the whole building. This results from the optimized ratio of building surface area to volume, which is also a measure of the compactness of a building. Reducing extended building energy demands requires no further energy-related measures because the largely highly insulated new building envelope of the vertical extension improves the energy balance of the whole building, even without the refurbished facades being taken into account. If a facade renovation also takes place, this further improves the energy-

efficiency of the building. The reuse of components and constructions from the existing building fabric provides the further advantage of savings in CO_2 emissions compared with demolition and new construction. The materials in the existing building can be reused without causing further emissions from manufacture. Likewise, the energy for the demolition is also saved.

Vertical extension vs. demolition/new construction

A recent study at Ruhr University Bochum (RUB) compared a project in which storeys were added with a fictitious demolition/new construction variant [5]. The comparison was based on life cycle analysis method adapted to the redesign of existing buildings (Fig. 4). The study shows that the embodied energy from the existing building offers potential advantages (Fig. 5). In the demolition/new construction variant, the entire structure was demolished and replaced with a new volume, its size and cubage matching the extension variant. In addition to the emissions from the new materials, the study also considered the improvements offered by a low-energy standard replacement

(Effizienzhaus 55 in concrete/masonry) over the period of observation.
The vertical extension variant was based on a previously completed project in which a building from the 1950s was refurbished to improve its energy efficiency with an external thermal insulation composite system (ETICS) and extended vertically with a prefabricated brick wall construction. The flat roof structure consists of timber. Both variants are connected to the district heating system. Using timber instead of brick for the vertical extension would further improve the result.
The study shows that adding storeys to the existing volume, including the manufacture of their material, causes less CO_2 emissions over the whole life cycle than the demolition/new construction variant. The greater emissions of the new structure at the time of manufacture cannot be amortized over the whole period of observation. The continued use of the existing materials, as well as avoiding the need for demolition and the remanufacture of new building materials, gives rise to significant savings in CO_2 emissions over the life cycle and incurs only about half the life cycle costs compared to demolition and new construction.

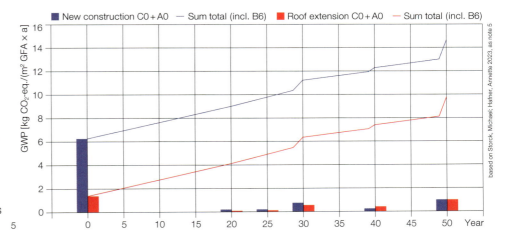

6   Increase of settlement and transportation area
    (from the German Federal Statistical Office).
    The land use survey is based on an analysis of
    the land register of the German federal states.
    The representation of the land use increase is
    skewed from 2004 due to the reorganization of
    land register data (the recoding of the and use
    types during digitalisation).
7   Construction cost comparison of adding storeys
    and new construction based on the ccst groups
    in DIN 276

Societal aspects

From a cultural and sociological point
of view, the retention and extension of
existing structures satisfies the needs
of a changing society. The greatest
development potential for densification
is offered by districts with established
urban residential structures from the
1950s. Originally, they would have been
on the edges of town but today they form
a considerable part of central urban
areas. The change in occupancy structure, e.g. the disappearance of multi-
generational households through children
moving away from their families and the
surge of single-person households, has
triggered a decline in the population of
the affected districts. Increasing prosper-
ity and expectations are further factors

that explain the rise of residential area
per capita over the last 30 years. Based
on the numbers, in late 2021 an individual
occupied an average of 47.7 m² of living
space comprising 2.3 habitable rooms. In
1991, the average was 34.9 m² of living
space and 1.8 habitable rooms per person. That represents a rise of the average
living space per capita of about 37 %
within 30 years. The average size of a
dwelling increased over this period from
82.1 m² to 92.1 m² [7].
In an ideal situation, by reducing the
average number of habitable rooms per
person and increasing the number of
inhabitants per m², adding storeys can
allow a functioning social structure to
grow. This may also lead to improvements,
such as by facilitating the revitalization
of a growing urban quarter through a

regulating mix of new housing units. The
increase in population density usually
leads to the establishment of service-
sector suppliers and local shops catering
to everyday needs. Adding storeys and
extensions to existing buildings contrib-
utes not only to the enhancement of the
quarter in terms of architecture and urban
design but also increases its desirability.
By adding storeys, it is also possible to
improve the flexibility of use of a building
and enliven its architectural appeal (Fig. 6).

Economic aspects

The German federal government's goal
as part of its national sustainability strategy is to reduce the rate at which land is
developed for new settlement and transportation purposes in Germany from the
current 55 ha/day to less than 30 ha/day,
followed by the long-term goal of the
integrated environmental programme [8]
of a reduction to 20 ha/day. The densification of residential and non-residential
buildings is a proven means of achieving
these goals.

Single- and two-family houses
In the view of the fact that of the 45
million housing units in Germany only
one half are to be found in multistorey
apartment complexes, there is also
a need to look at the other half, the
single- and two-family houses, in order
to do justice to this topic.
According to the position paper [9] by
Thomas Auer and Andreas Hild, single-
family houses have an enormous surplus
of space and a high level of service from
the associated infrastructure. According
to the study by Kevin Anderson from the
University of Manchester mentioned in
the paper, the CO_2 emissions per person
for daily living and transport purposes
(including the grey emissions required

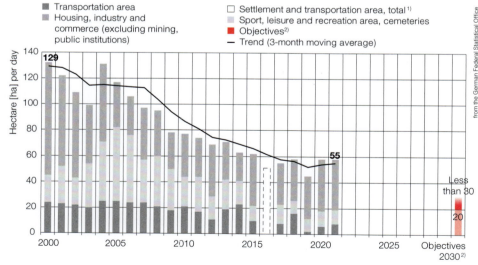

from the German Federal Statistical Office

1) The differentiation between "buildings and urban open space" and "industrial/commercial sites not
including mining land" ceases from 2016 because of the system change from the Automated Property
Register (ALB) to the automated Official Land Registry Information System (ALKIS). This adversely
affects comparisons based on time and makes the calculation of changes more difficult. The settlement and transportation infrastructure category after the system change generally contains the same
land use types as it did before.
2) Objectives by 2030: Reduction to under 30 ha per day (German Sustainable Development Strategy,
new edition 2016); 20 ha per day (Integrated Environment Programme 2030)

6

Notes
[1] United Nations Environment Programme: 2020 Global Status Report for Buildings and Construction – Towards a Zero-emission, Efficient and Resilient Buildings and Construction Sector. Nairobi 2020
[2] The Royal Academy of Engineering: Engineering a Low Carbon Built Environment. The Discipline of Building Engineering Physics. London 2010
[3] Tichelmann, Karsten et al.: Deutschlandstudie 2019 Wohnraumpotenziale in urbanen Lagen – Aufstockung und Umnutzung von Nichtwohngebäuden, TU Darmstadt, ISP Eduard Pestel Institut 2019
[4] Tichelmann, Karsten; Groß, Katrin; Günther, Matthias: Deutschlandstudie 2015. Wohnraumpotenziale durch Aufstockungen. TU Darmstadt, ISP Eduard Pestel Institut 2016
[5] Storck, Michael; Hafner, Annette: Aufstockung versus Abriss und Neubau – Vergleich von ökologischen und ökonomischen Auswirkungen. Bauphysik Kalender 2023. Weinheim 2023
[6] Hafner, Annette et al.: Holz in der Aufstockung – Bewertung und Umsetzung von Holz in Aufstockungsmaßnahmen. Final report: 2220HV004A/B. BMEL/FNR. Berlin/Gülzow 2024
[7] Statistisches Bundesamt (Destatis): Press release No. N041, 29 June 2023
[8] Statistisches Bundesamt (Destatis): Press release Zahl der Woche No. 09, 28.2.2023
[9] Auer, Thomas; Hild, Andreas: Vom Schmuddelkind zum Hoffnungsträger. Position paper. 28.3.2023
[10] As note 3

for them) in rural areas is twice as high as in cities. The reason is that the buildings and the infrastructure experience below-average utilization. The embodied grey energy and the resources in areas in which there are mainly single-family houses therefore offer enormous hidden potential for adding storeys and extensions. Implementation of such projects, however, is often limited by planning policies and building laws. In areas with mainly single-family houses, it may be possible for densification to counteract the social and cultural effects of having increasingly high percentages of elderly people. In the course of the additions, the newly created living space could also be better balanced in terms of the different age groups, such as by adding smaller housing units that better meet the needs of older people. Multiple generations living under the same roof can improve the social environment in the building and in the district.

In contrast to new construction, extending vertically has the economic benefit that the necessary infrastructure and transport links are already available, while soil sealing and coverage of surrounding areas are prevented. This saves a large proportion of the land that would otherwise be consumed by a comparable new structure. The Deutschlandstudie 2019 (see "Densification strategies", p. 49f.) also examined how much land could potentially be saved by adding storeys and extensions. The results showed that densification by building in the existing stock in regions with higher housing demands could avoid land consumption ranging from 110 million m^2 (slab housing development) to 250 million m^2 (mixed urban development) to provide impervious surfaces for buildings, communal open spaces and land used for transport purposes [10].

Double inward urban growth
In terms of double inward urban growth, which has the aim of securing communal green spaces on public land, adding roof extensions to existing buildings makes an important contribution through their minimal footprint. Additional roof areas, especially if flat, offer potential for introducing green roofs. In combination with green facades, they can counter temporary overheating of urban microclimates due to climate change based on allowing rainwater stored in the vegetation to evaporate.

Communal roof gardens provide a communication space for residents, who may also actively participate in urban gardening, and represent social added value for the people living in multi-family houses (see the example of the "Housing complex in Salzburg", p. 50f.).

Sharing existing supply structures and costs
In addition to the existing communal circulation and mobility areas, the building's public utilities supply structure can be adapted and extended. As a rule, the entrance areas and the circulation routes inside the building can be shared and used. Additional foundations and earthworks are unnecessary in most cases. Out of all this can arise valuable, often highly attractive living space. Sharing the operating costs of the building among an increased number of parties can even lead to added value in an economic sense for all the residents. The increase in living space offsets the cost of refurbishment in financial terms (Fig. 7).

Lift shaft, if required
CG 500 Exteriors
CG 400 Services

Renovation and construction, if required
CG 300 Construction works

CG 200 Clearance and development
CG 100 Site

From Deutschlandstudie 2019, as note 3

7   **Vertical extension**   **Cost groups DIN 276**   **New construction**

Vertical Extensions in Timber

Manfred Stieglmeier

Building with timber is extremely suitable for adapting existing stock and particularly so for adding storeys in vertical extensions. Due to its special material properties, low weight, high load-bearing capability and good insulating effect, timber is ideal for meeting the requirements of building in existing stock. In addition to the structural and building physics advantages of timber construction, another good reason for adding storeys in this sustainable raw material is the fact that CO_2 is stored in the installed wood (see "The Social Challenges of Building", p. 7ff.).

The low weight of timber

The load-bearing capacity reserves of an existing structure and therefore the allowable weight of the new structure are crucial when considering adding one or more storeys to a building. In contrast to mineral construction materials, timber is both lightweight and capable of carrying high loads. Lightweight timber frame wall elements or cross-laminated timber walls are able to transmit loads from the additional storeys transversely to the principal supporting axis of the existing structure, which allows architects to create flexible room layouts. If the load-bearing capacity of the top-storey ceiling construction is inadequate, particularly in the case of residential buildings of the post-war period, one solution is to replace it with a lightweight construction such as a cross-laminated timber or hollow box floor. An assessment of the existing building and its components is essential for the structural calculation of the transmission of the applied loads from the additional storeys into the existing structure. Fig. 1 provides examples of different wall cross sections having the same U-value and clearly demonstrates the weight advantages of timber over other types of construction. The self-weight of a timber frame wall is

ca. 43 % of a masonry wall made from perforated clay bricks and ca. 31 % of a reinforced concrete wall.

Advantages of prefabrication

Prefabrication greatly increases the potential of using modern timber construction for building in existing contexts. Konrad Wachsmann described the process as a "principle of industrialization that requires the production facilities to move from the building site or the workshop into the factory" [1]. This considerably shortens installation time on site and reduces noise and disturbance from site activities, which is particularly beneficial in an urban environment. With the help of modern transport and site logistics, even large-format wall and floor elements can be installed in congested inner-city surroundings without having to employ costly site equipment. Prefabrication in the factory and rapid installation also reduce the risk of moisture damage from rain and bad weather during the construction phase.

Work to install additional storeys often has to take place without interrupting building operation and therefore requires carefully planned and smoothly executed construction processes. This is best achieved by low-emission and extremely quick assembly of the components on site. Prefabrication of building elements therefore provides solutions that can be implemented without much noise, with high precision and within a short construction period. There are also economic advantages arising from prefabrication because the building users do not have to leave their familiar surroundings and temporarily move into other premises. In the case of school buildings for example, the summer holidays are frequently long enough to complete the installation of the wood construction elements and the waterproofing work, which is an advantage that would

1 Weight comparison of common wall components per m² for the same U-value of 0.196 W/m²K
   a Timber frame wall
   b Reinforced concrete wall
   c Masonry wall of perforated brick
2 Three-storey addition in timber construction, Rauti-Huus, Zurich (CH) 1948/2016, Spillmann Echsle Architekten
   a Grid of new steel beams and existing deck support structure
   b The addition has three storeys, with the lowest level concealed behind the redesigned facade of the fourth floor. The two-storey part in the recognizable roof addition contains maisonette dwellings.

Timber frame wall:
15 mm OSB board, 202 mm spruce solid construction timber/cellulose insulation, 18 mm gypsum fibreboard, windtight layer, 30/50 mm vertical and horizontal battens, 72/23 mm external wall cladding
Total weight: 352.28 kN/m²

Reinforced concrete wall:
20 mm render, 16 mm rigid foam (XPS 040), 250 mm reinforced concrete, 15 mm plaster
Total weight: 1133.32 kN/m²

Masonry wall:
20 mm render, 200 mm hollow brick 1400 kg/m³, 14.7 mm rigid foam (XPS 040), 15 mm plaster
Total weight: 814.36 kN/m²

1

2 a   b

not be available with conventional building methods.

Vertical extension for flats in Zurich

The advantages of timber construction are made obvious by the example of the Rauti-Huus, a former factory in Zurich built in 1948. The building features four full storeys and a recessed rooftop floor and had recently housed offices and laboratories. Spillmann Echsle Architekten designed a timber structure as roof extension with 17 new housing units covering 94 to 140 m². This was possible by the activation of an existing 30% land use reserve for the allowable floor area. The addition is comprised of three storeys, with the lowest of the additional storeys concealed behind the redesigned facade of the fourth floor. The two-storey volume that rests on the former roofline, a playful arrangement of interconnected cubes, is clearly recognizable as an addition. It comprises generous loft spaces organized as maisonette apartments with private roof terraces.. All the housing units are connected by an internal corridor on the fourth floor.

The existing concrete structure is loaded to a significant degree of its capacity, which required the loads to be applied evenly to the 70 cm thick concrete columns, arranged 5 m off centre along the central axis of the building. A central beam running along the whole 60 m length of the structure at the level of the third floor distributes the loads. A grid of steel beams was installed between the slender concrete columns of the facade and the central beam. At the outer wall, the grid is supported on neoprene bearings to distribute the loads evenly onto the 12 × 20 cm facade columns. The vertical addition comprises three new storeys consisting of wood frame and solid timber elements with structural cross-laminated timber walls designed as shear

walls to transmit the loads directly into the load distribution system. The new floors are designed as hollow boxes equipped with cement boards in their interiors in order to achieve the required sound insulation values.

Timber construction not only promises low weight but also short on-site construction times due to prefabrication in the workshop and the itemized delivery of elements. Installation of the windows and facade elements takes place on site. Transport constraints meant that the size of the elements for the hollow box floors was limited to 2.50 × 13 m. They were prefabricated to include fire resistant cladding, insulation and the inlaid cement boards. The extension of the existing building by creating additional storeys was completed without interrupting daily operations on the floors below.

Applications and advantages of vertical extensions

The scope of timber construction elements suitable for existing buildings ranges from individual parts, such as purlins, columns and beams for replacing or supplementing individual building components, to prefabricated timber frame wall elements for walls and roofs. Complete room modules offer the highest degree of prefabrication particularly for extensions and additional storeys if groups of rooms of the same configuration and functional units are repeated multiple times (see "Room modules", p. 68f.). Proven design solutions for new construction can be applied in timber as well. CNC production technology, which is now in widespread use in the industry, allows even complex, three-dimensional, customized and highly thermally insulated components to be serially manufactured for timber frame wall or room modules. The high degree of stiffness of modules also allows them to bridge relatively long spans in existing structures. Advantages of timber

construction in existing buildings [2]:
With respect to structural design:
- Lightweight construction (especially suitable for existing buildings with limited load-bearing reserves)
- Load distribution can be designed specifically for the existing structure – even for long spans

With respect to construction:
- Fully planned construction flow
- High degree of prefabrication
- Progress largely unaffected by the seasons
- High precision and quality

With respect to architectural design:
- No limits to design freedom in relation to form, facade and interior design, although the dimensions of the components need to be adjusted to suit site circumstances and transport constraints

With respect to logistics:
- Rapid construction from a high degree of prefabrication
- Disturbance to the surroundings minimized by rapid construction
- Construction can continue with the building still operating
- No construction equipment permanently required on site (an otherwise high cost item)

With respect to sustainability:
- Prolonged life cycle of the existing building
- Wood is a climate-neutral construction material
- The structure can be dismantled and reused (perhaps elsewhere)

Notes
[1] Wachsmann, Konrad: Wendepunkt im Bauen. Wiesbaden 1959
[2] Lattke, Frank: Weiterbauen mit Holz. In: Zuschnitt No. 66, 2017, p. 7

Building Alterations and Protection of Existing Property Rights

Thomas Engel, Manfred Stieglmeier

Building law framework conditions

Adding storeys usually changes the volume and geometry of a building. The requirements under the planning legislation for the region must be identified and followed during the whole project. Determinations under planning legislation are frequently governed by planning law and land use planning in the form of the land use plan and by municipal regulations. These types of determinations include, in particular, the proportion of a plot of land that can be used for building development and the rules on setbacks between buildings. In the case of adding storeys without related land use plan, the permissibility of the measures ia governed by § 34 of the German Federal Building Code (Baugesetzbuch, BauGB). The characteristic feature of the project's immediate environment determines the type of construction and the extent of use for building. Further requirements are governed by the federal state-specific building regulations or by the model building regulations (MBO).

The example of the Deutscher Alpenverein (DAV) headquarters shows the transformation of an existing building according to a new form of architectural expression and the associated change of the building volume (Fig. 3, p. 59, see "Deutscher Alpenverein (DAV) Headquarters, Munich", p. 69).

Setbacks

A change of the building volume as a result of adding storeys in most cases also changes the building height. Because the vertical dimensions of the whole of the building are the basis for setback regulations [1], the influence of the additional storeys with respect to whether the measures can be approved must be investigated (Fig. 2).

Vehicle parking spaces

The number of required parking spaces for a building project is typically determined in accordance with the relevant federal state building regulations or a municipal parking space code. In the case of building in an existing context, it may often be the case that the existing building has no parking spaces. However, in most cases, these are provided additionally by interventions in the building fabric or are subject to a payment in lieu of the required parking places.

Passenger lifts

Installation of a passenger lift is obligatory above a certain building height, which may vary and is determined by the applicable building regulations. In accordance with §39 MBO, lifts of an adequate size and number must be provided above a building height of 13 m (Fig. 1). If there are no lifts in the existing building, they are usually required as an addition. Up to building class 4, a lift shaft may be fitted in the stairwell or on the outside of the building. In the case of adding storeys with the intent of creating residential space, a lift can be omitted if the work and expense involved would be disproportionate.

Accessibility

At the time they were built, measures to ensure accessibility were not relevant to most of today's existing buildings in urban areas. When adding storeys, it is therefore always necessary to clarify the fulfilment of accessibility requirements. In accordance with §50 of the MBO, a new building with more than two dwellings requires barrier-free access for all housing units per floor. Within the dwelling, at least one lavatory and one bathroom must be accessible, as must the kitchen, living rooms and bedrooms. If further dwellings result from the addition of up to

1 Regulations concerning the installation of passenger lifts in accordance with the federal state building regulations
2 Types of additional storeys and the typical effects on setbacks between buildings

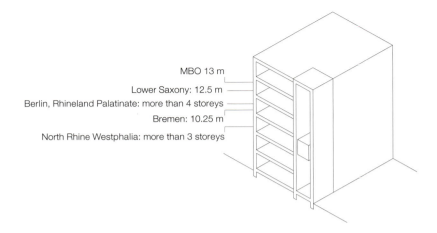

MBO 13 m
Lower Saxony: 12.5 m
Berlin, Rhineland Palatinate: more than 4 storeys
Bremen: 10.25 m
North Rhine Westphalia: more than 3 storeys

1

two storeys or the construction of a roof storey, this regulation does not apply.

Listed buildings

Adding storeys involves changing the appearance of architecture. Therefore, the historic preservation status of a listed building or group of buildings must be investigated at the start of the planning process, in particular for structures from the mid-late 1800s, 1920s and 1930s. The provisions of the listed status may in some instances affect only part of the existing building fabric. In this context, adding storeys may be permissible on a case-by-case basis.

Thermal insulation

Interventions in the existing fabric by adding storeys that lead to replacing major parts of a building structure significantly impact the thermal envelope. In terms of building law, they no longer comprise minor measures. Thermal insulation is governed by the federal state building regulations and must be verified during the design of the project. The German Buildings Energy Act (GEG) also sets other mandatory requirements. Part 3 of the GEG, which came into force in 2020, details the requirements for an

existing building subject to alteration and extension. In the case of changes made to external building components covering more than 10 % of a component group, the requirements for thermal transmittance are set out in Appendix 7. The precise guidance values for extensions such as additional storeys are also given in GEG Part 3. In accordance with Appendix 3, the transmission heat loss for residential buildings is limited to 1.2 times that of the reference building. For non-residential buildings the limit for the average U-value is 1.25 times the reference value. The primary energy demand for extensions is to be calculated only in the case of non-residential buildings with an extension floor area of more than 100 % of the existing building area.

If the heat source is replaced or an additional heat source added, then the requirements of GEG Part 4 are to be determined in accordance with the current provisions of the legislation at the time. According to this, the basic requirement is that at least 65 % of the heat provided must be generated using renewable energy or unavoidable waste heat. In addition, numerous interim regulations and exceptions may apply.

Protection of existing property rights

The principle of protecting existing property rights (e.g. by grandfathering) is contained in Art. 14 (1) of the German Basic Law (GG) [2]. This protection under building law concerns the right of owners to continue to retain and use a physical structure connected to a specific use that was legal, or at least was formally legalized by having been granted a building permit at the time of its construction. This is also the case if erecting a building would no longer be permissible following changes in legal requirements. "Building law assumes that, for legally built or modified structures, the material regulations applicable to its construction or modification continue to be binding. Later material regulations of the federal state building code are in principle not to be applied to structures that were legally constructed or modified before the later material regulations came into force." [3] A physical structure [4] is protected in this way if:
- It was granted a building permit and constructed in compliance with its permit ("formal grandfathering")
- It complied with the applicable law at the time it was built ("material grandfathering") and

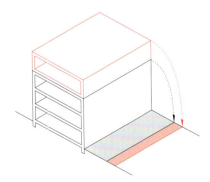
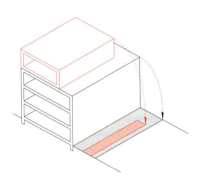
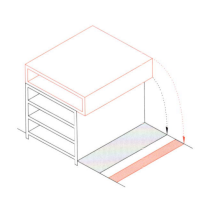

2

Schematic drawing based on Fabian Jäger, 2019

- Since then has not been modified in a manner that did not comply with the law

Protection of existing property rights is applicable to buildings independently of whether their construction is legally compliant or not in formal and/or material terms. This is also the case if construction corresponded to material law at the time and according to when the building inspection assessment took place (e.g. decision on building application or building inspection measures) [5]. Grandfathering is distinguished according to its active and passive forms.

Active grandfathering

Active protection of existing property rights (active grandfathering) applies to an extension of an existing building [6]. The legal existence of a physical structure entitles the owner to carry out measures that would not be permissible under the currently applicable law [7]. The extent of this entitlement depends on the measure to be permitted: If it comprises repair or maintenance work, it is called simple active grandfathering. On the other hand, if the measure is intended to extend the existing building, then this is termed "overarching" grandfathering because it is covered by the protection applicable to of the other parts of the structure [8].

Passive grandfathering

With passive grandfathering, the protection of existing property rights comes to bear passively: It protects the status quo against changes in the law. As long as the identity of the building is maintained, the traditional interpretation of passive grandfathering also allows maintenance work within narrow limits [9]. The following basic rules apply: if a physical structure is protected by grandfathering, then in terms of building law it is not necessary to continually retrofit the structure in order

to adhere to currently applicable regulations. However, grandfathering ends if a situation arises that is not covered by the building permit. One such loss of grandfathering can be caused by the following construction measures [10]:
- Improper placement of cables or wires through walls and floors detrimentally affecting fire resistance of these components
- Interference with escape routes by the later installation of partition walls, access controls etc.
- Creation of habitable rooms in the basement without the required escape routes
- Substantial increase in the number of persons exceeding the capacity of escape routes
- Changes to the exteriors and therefore possibly also to space required for fire-fighting

Grandfathering in practice

For alterations or changes of use of existing buildings, the applicable building regulation requirements must be observed. They relate to all measures under consideration insofar they can be distinguished as such. However, they don't generally apply to areas not subject to a measure, or the entire building [11].

If, as part of the proposed measure, certain requirements cannot be met due to the physical circumstances of the existing structure (e.g. the connection of new fire-resisting walls and floors to components of the existing building that do not have the required fire rating stipulated by the current versions of the relevant technical rules), then actual circumstances require evaluation. This can indicate whether deviating from preconditions stated by respective building codes is permissible. Such deviations are permissible if no concerns are raised that require revisiting basic aspects of the permit process.

If the measure is purely a change of use without structural intervention, then whether and to what extent it raises a new concern relating to official approval by the planning and building authorities should be evaluated. Depending on the circumstances, it is also possible to separately consider the situation with respect to structural integrity and fire protection. Examples:
- For a change of use from an office to a school, the concerns usually raised relate to the structural integrity and fire protection (escape route layout).
- On the other hand, for a change of use from housing to offices there are usually no fundamental concerns raised relating to fire protection. However, the floors will be subject to a different set of applied loads.

In the case of a significant change to an existing building that raises new concerns relating to official approval by the planning and building authorities but is limited to a specific definable area within the building, an adaptation of the entire existing building to the applicable law is generally not required [12].

The approving authority can demand that parts not affected by changes are made compliant with legal standards binding at the time, if safety concerns require it. This is the case if demands are economically feasible for the client and parts not affected by changes are linked to or connected with parts subject to changes in terms of their construction. This applies in particular in the presence of "significant danger". One such instance arises in relation to fire protection if the two independent escape routes required for habitable rooms are not present at all or if there is only one escape route and it has significant deficits. A significant danger in this sense arises, however, not just because the legal regulations have changed over the course of time [13]. In order to determine whether a significant danger is present, an assessment of the actual situation on site is always necessary. Examples:

- In the case of a general refurbishment of an office building with changes that require approval in many different areas, the approval authorities may demand that the doors in the adjoining parts of the complex are brought up to the currently applicable requirements.
- When converting the attic of an existing building into habitable space or extending it, parts subject to change (attic) and parts not subject to change (e.g. entrance doors to existing apartments) feature neither direct (built) links nor construction-based connections. In most of these cases, retrofitting doors in the walls of necessary stairwells is not required.

Conclusion
A roof conversion project typically does not involve any changes that raise new concerns relating to official approval by the planning and building authorities. A roof extension that leads to increased

height can potentially result in a new building class designation and, thus, comprises a significant change that calls for revisiting the approval process. This requires case-by-case consideration and evaluation whether material deviations are justified or not.

Object-based protection status assessment
In order to assess the grandfathering status of a building, all relevant documents must be collated and evaluated. These include, in particular:

- The notification granting the building permit
- The drawings relating to the permit
- Fire protection certification report
- Records of communications with the building and fire authorities

Details of earlier processes can be reviewed in the files kept by the building authority. Other useful archives include local government and federal state records. If there are no documents available, or they are incomplete or inconclusive, the grandfathering status can be assessed by considering the building law applicable at that time.

3 Raising the height of the building by adding storeys and extensions here represents a significant change that raises new concerns relating to official approval by the planning and building authorities. Rooftop addition and extension, headquarters of the Deutscher Alpenverein (DAV), Munich (DE) 2021, ELEMENT A. Architekten, hiendl_ schineis architektenpartnerschaft
a Appearance of the building before the extension: reinforced concrete structure from the 1970s
b Transformation with the new building envelope in combination with additional storeys and an extension

Notes
[1] [1] Fath, Maren et al.: Leitlinie zur Vereinfachung der Planung und Durchführung von Aufstockungs- / Erweiterungsmaßnahmen als Nachverdichtungsmaßnahme in innerstädtischen Bereichen. Stuttgart 2019
[2] Basic Law of the German Federal Republic (GG): Article 14(1)
[3] Molodovsky, Paul; Famers, Gabriele; Waldmann, Timm: Kommentar – Bayerische Bauordnung, Art. 54 BauO BY, 148th update. Munich / Heidelberg 2023
[4] Oberste Baubehörde im Bayerischen Staatsministerium des Innern: Vollzug der Bayerischen Bauordnung (BayBO); Brandschutz in bestehenden Gebäuden. 2011. IIB7-4112.420-013/11
[5] As note 3
[6] Sendler, Horst: Bestandsschutz im Wirtschaftsleben. In: WiVerw 1993
[7] Friauf, Karl Heinrich: Bestandsschutz bei gewerblichen Anlagen. In: Bachhof, Otto; Heigl, Ludwig; Redeker, Konrad (pub.): Festgabe aus Anlass des 25jährigen Bestehens des Bundesverwaltungsgerichts. Munich 1978, p. 220
[8] Michl, Fabian: Der baurechtliche Bestandsschutz zwischen Grundgesetz und einfachem Recht. In: ThürVBl. issue 12/2010
[9] ibid.
[10] As note 4
[11] ibid.
[12] ibid.
[13] HessVGH: Beschl. v. 18.10.1999 – 4 TG 3007/97

3a   b

Vertical Extension Typologies and Conversion Culture

Manfred Stieglmeier

Conversion culture

Over recent years, building in existing stock has established itself alongside new construction as an equally demanding design task. The focus is no longer merely on the energy-efficiency modernization required by regulations but also the transformation of the building envelope. This allows creating an entirely new architectural expression in the respective context. This existing fabric is the material and the architectural resource for buildings of the future. The deliberation on the effect of place on architecture is, thus, not limited to new construction. The further development of the existing fabric persistently stimulates the interactions between buildings and their surroundings. Spatial situations assume a new character when buildings or block borders receive roof extensions. In urban design terms, they often contribute to restructuring and improving the spatial context by contouring streets, places or settlement structures and providing them with a sense of identity. Building in existing stock leads to a conversion culture that extends beyond simply adding storeys and purely economic considerations to include aspects of urban design and architecure. Conversions can also have social and cultural effects, such as restructuring the social mix of district residents or supplying infrastructure to meet neighbourhood needs, e.g. new businesses and service providers (see "Societal aspects", p. 52).

Roof extensions

With the transformation of the spatial configuration and external appearance, the converted building inevitably reacts to the established structure of the surroundings. The formulation of the geometric shape of the roof can accommodate a range of architectural requirements. Additional height, projections or recesses change the character of the building and its spatial effect on the surroundings. Frequently, the architectural design is determined by the historical context or building culture. Although the simple attic conversion in which the roof structure is retained or strengthened to support more effective thermal insulation is the simplest form of roof renewal, there are hardly any limits to architectural design freedom with respect to form and materialization when extending vertically. The scope and type of vertical extension are defined by the legal framework, the setbacks between buildings and the extent of use of the plot by the building (see "Public building law – legal framework", p. 56f.). By the redesign of the existing stock, the building and the context are invigorated, deficiencies in the original architecture are rectified or standards are raised, for example, by providing barrier-free access, spaces for common use in the form of extensions, or improvements in usability by adding loggias or informal meeting places in the roof area.

Example – roof extension in Berlin
The roof extension of the Berlin Metropolitan School designed by architects Sauerbruch Hutton is an example of the formal diversity that can be achieved by adding storeys (Fig. 2). The external wall of the roof extension leans outwards due to the joint of the roof truss frame being positioned beyond the edge of the roof and towards the internal courtyard, which the building borders on three sides. The materials selection features sheet copper that contrasts with the tectonic character of the prefabricated reinforced concrete panels of the No. 80 school type from 1987 (SBR 80, Erfurt), which features a single-loaded corridor. Prefabrication of the components for the single and in some areas double storey extension of the block border structure allowed

1 Vertical extension typology: different geometries for additional storeys
2 Roof construction in solid timber on a precast panel system building from 1987, copper external skin. Roof extension, Berlin Metropolitan School, Berlin (DE) 2020, Sauerbruch Hutton
3 Urban densification, roof extension on a multi-storey car park, children's day-care centre, Nuremberg (DE) 2015, Querwärts Architekten

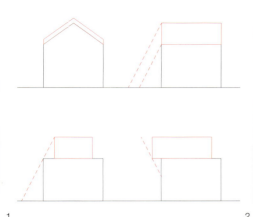

1

2

3

construction to proceed while school operations were ongoing. The minimal self-weight of the new roof construction meant that no additional foundations or structural components for the load-bearing system of the existing precast panel building were necessary.

Vertical extension typologies

The Deutschlandstudie 2019 [1] describes the potential for creating new living space by adding storeys to existing buildings for four main typologies (see "Potential of Vertical Extensions", p. 49ff.).

Adding storeys to multi-family residential buildings
Multi-family residential blocks constructed between 1950 and 1989 comprise the major part of Germany's present-day housing stock in urban areas and provide the ideal basis for roof extensions [2]. The shallow depths of residential buildings from the 1950s make them particularly suitable for extending vertically. An analysis of the reserve load-bearing capacity by building type in the study showed that the construction related preconditions are fulfilled for adding storeys to existing stock designed and built to earlier codes of practice and building standards. From the point of view of energy, adding storeys above the current top floor can be expected to reduce the energy required for heating by up to 50%.

Adding storeys to non-residential buildings: retail
Most single-storey standardized retail facilities can be found in urban districts on valuable plots that offer great potential for densification projects. In particular, parking space occupies a large share of area no longer accessible to uses of higher value, such as housing. Single-storey buildings are somewhat less suitable for roof extensions because their load reserve

is smaller. The potential for further development here lies much more in building replacements with an extended range of integrated uses or erecting raised structures above parking lots.

Administration buildings
Offices and administration buildings are currently subject to significant processes of change. Flexible working practices such as co-working or remote work demand alternative concepts from a workplace. Traditional places of work may often lack the potential for redesigning them accordingly. This makes sites available for further development for housing or other uses. In Germany, currently 6.5% of office space is no longer used as such [3]. The buildings affected are mainly those from the 1950s to the 1980s. In contrast to housing construction, offices and administration buildings frequently have a load-bearing skeleton frame that is independent of the fire-separating wall constructions, and therefore they can be flexibly configured for a variety of different uses. In Germany, ca. 300,000 office and administration buildings have the potential for a change of use in combination with additional storeys (see Deutscher Alpenverein (DAV) Headquarters, Munich, p. 69).

Non-residential buildings: parking garages
Due to the car-friendly urban planning schemes of the 1970s inner cities are still defined by multistorey parking garages, even on high-value properties. Although the parking spaces within them have no shortage of users, rooftop parking lots are less frequented. These outdoor spaces are, however, ideally suited for rooftop extensions because multistorey parking garages usually have adequate load-bearing reserves to support additional storeys. Such new spaces offer potential for social uses, an example of

which is the children's day care centre by Querwärts Architekten in Nuremberg (Fig. 3). The idea of establishing a children's day care centre at a height of 16.70 m above the ground sounded risky. Eventually, however, the lack of social welfare provisions and available land in the area of the site due to the high-density development resulted in its transformation into a rooftop extension with a lightweight timber panel construction. The extra storeys are placed on the southern half of the concrete structure and therefore leave a large area of the former rooftop parking deck free as an outdoor playground for the 86 children, who are divided into four groups. A lift provides access and is also used by the fire brigade in the event of a fire.

Wood was the material chosen for the project because of its low weight and the short installation time made possible by the high degree of prefabrication. The project was completed within nine months. When planning began, it was necessary to increase the load-bearing reserves of the existing structure, which was achieved by removing and disposing of 700 t of surface material from the parking garage rooftop level. The new roof construction is a combination of extensive and intensive greening as well as child-friendly play zones with pavers on top of a bituminous waterproofing membrane on the reinforced concrete slab. Finally, it was even possible to plant trees in certain areas supported by retrofit existing downstand beams.

Notes
[1] Tichelmann, Karsten et. al: Deutschlandstudie 2019. Wohnraumpotenziale in urbanen Lagen – Aufstockung und Umnutzung von Nichtwohngebäuden. TU Darmstadt/ISP Eduard Pestel Institut 2019
[2] Tichelmann, Karsten; Groß, Katrin; Günther, Matthias: Deutschlandstudie 2015. Wohnraumpotenziale durch Aufstockungen TU Darmstadt/ISP Eduard Pestel Institut 2016
[3] As note 1

Fire Protection for Vertical Extensions

Thomas Engel

WSH ≤ 23 m
FFL ≤ 22 m

Fire brigade aerial rescue vehicle (turntable ladder)

WSH ≤ 8 m
FFL ≤ 7 m

Portable ladder (sectional ladder)

1

Building classes

In all German federal state building codes, buildings are distinguished into five different building classes (GK) according to their height, specifically the height of the finished floor level (FFL) of the highest occupied storey above the average ground surface level, and the size of an occupancy unit (OU). When designing a vertical extension to a building, it should be noted that adding storeys may lead to a different building class denomination and, in some circumstances, it may therefore need to meet other requirements (see "Public building law – legal framework", p. 56f.). A higher building class is subject to higher requirements under building regulations in order to fulfil the necessary level of safety. Buildings with a height of less than 7 m are classified as GK 1–3, while buildings between 7 m and 13 m high and with occupancy units smaller than 400 m² are class GK 4. Other buildings, including underground structures, fall into class GK 5 (Fig. 3).

In addition to standard buildings, there are also structures designated as so-called "special building" ("Sonderbau") cases for a variety of reasons. Special buildings need to fulfil different safety standards because of their particular type or use (e.g. high-rise buildings, hospitals, schools). The precise definition of what constitutes a special building case is provided by building regulations. The building class, however, is considered independently of the status as special building case. Thus, e.g. a very tall building (elevation above topmost FFL > 22 m) is classified as GK 5 while a two-storey building (elevation above topmost FFL ≤ 7 m, > 2 OU) with a nursery school on the ground floor is classified as GK 3 and then additionally identified as a special building. A building is designated as a special building case if, for example, it poses

special risks to the users because they are not fully mobile (e.g. hospital, nursing home) or are vulnerable in other ways. High numbers of people (e.g. football stadium) or unusual circumstances that present the fire brigade with problems, e.g. the time required to reach the fire and access difficulties (e.g. high-rise buildings), are two reasons for this designation.

Escape and rescue routes

Escape and rescue routes enable building users to escape (or be rescued by others) and provide access routes for firefighting. The following special requirements apply to these designated movement routes. Escape routes allow people to escape to a safe area in the event of fire. Escape routes may include, for example, designated fire stairwells, fire corridors and fire exits to the open air. Escape routes within buildings are designed for people to move from inside to outside. Rescue routes, on the other hand, are there to provide safe access for fire service rescue personnel moving from outside to inside. These access routes allow people (and animals) to be rescued by people other than themselves. In building legislation, escape and rescue routes may be referred to collectively under the single term "means of egress" (MoE).

In accordance with the building code, occupied rooms must always have two independent means of egress. As a result, should one means of egress be unavailable, the other can be used. The primary means of egress must always be protected by construction-based measures. In the case of multistorey buildings, this must be done by providing a designated fire stair in a fire stairwell with an exit to the open air. Fire stairwells enable people within buildings to evacuate before fire or smoke penetrates the

1 Overview of fire brigade ladders (WSH = window sill height , FFL = finished floor level)
2 Void between the new floor slab and the existing roof
  a Arrangement of fire protective cladding to protect the timber components in the void (building services storey)
  b Void completely filled (building services storey) with non-combustible insulation (melting point > 1000 °C) to prevent the spread of fire
3 Assignment of building classes in accordance with building regulations (FFL = finished floor level of highest possible occupied rooms above the average ground surface level, OU = occupancy unit)
4 Options for provision of means of egress in relation to height

1 Load-bearing
 existing wall
2 Roof slab (existing)
3 New floor of roof
 extension
4 New full-height roof
extension storey
5 Fire protective
 cladding
6 Non-combustible
 insulation (melting
 point > 1000 °C)

2 a   b

3

Building class 1	Building class 2	Building class 3	Building class 4	Building class 5
Detached building FFL ≤ 7 m ≤ 2 OU with total floor area ≤ 400 m² or agricultural building	FFL ≤ 7 m ≤ 2 OU with floor ≤ 400 m²	FFL ≤ 7 m > 2 OU	FFL > 7 m FFL ≤ 13 m OU < 400 m²	FFL > 13 m

≤ 7 m   ≤ 7 m   ≤ 7 m   ≤ 13 m   > 13 m

fire stairwells. The building components used must therefore be sufficiently fire-resistant. For a typical standard building (e.g. residential building), the secondary means of egress can be provided either as a construction-based means of egress or by the fire brigade's rescue equipment. For buildings up to and including GK 3, a portable four-section ladder may be employed, while a fire brigade aerial rescue vehicle (turntable ladder) (Fig. 1) is required for buildings of GK 4 and 5 below the high-rise limit. In planning it is necessary to ensure that required rescue equipment is available to local firefighters and the use and configuration of the building permits rescuing occupants by these means.

In terms of building code, for special buildings in which the secondary means of egress is to take place via fire brigade rescue equipment, it should typically be verified that there are no reservations about rescuing people in this way. This type of means of egress is not required if a stairwell is constructed in such a way that fire and smoke cannot penetrate it, and the means of egress is therefore a permanently usable and so-called smoke-proof enclosure. For high-rise buildings (elevation of FFL > 22 m), the second means of egress must always be protected by construction-based measures because heights above 23 m cannot be reached by typical fire brigade aerial rescue equipment. Fig. 4 shows the feasible options for providing a means of egress depending on the building height for structures with common types of use (e.g. residential or office use). The rules for the design of smokeproof enclosure are defined for the most part by high-rise guidelines. Some German federal states have different rules for smokeproof enclosure of standard buildings. An overview of these requirements can be found in the publication "Teilbericht Brandschutz

zum Forschungsvorhaben Extra Hohe Häuser" [1].

Vertical extensions can present problems in providing means of egress that comply with building law. This is particularly the case if potential areas required by fire-fighters in the context of the vertical extension can't be planned according to specifications. In these circumstances, customized solutions can be devised that appropriately compensate for the material departures from the requirements of the applicable federal state building codes. Possible concepts for evaluating frequently occurring deviations in connection with roof extensions can be found in the above-mentioned research projects [2].

Roof slab becomes the floor of the roof extension

Building law principally states no requirements for roof load-bearing structures or roof slabs (flat roof), except for the upper enclosure of necessary stairwells. Requirements for fire resistance of the roof slab can arise only from the connection to the partition walls of the top storey. Therefore, it can typically be assumed

that existing flat roofs don't feature a fire resistance rating. In the case of a proposed new roof extension, the fire performance of these floors must be appropriately modernized. It may be possible, for example, to install a new floor above the existing roof and have the floor supported on the existing load-bearing walls or on downstand beams and columns (Fig. 2). Ducts, pipes or cables would usually pass the void between the existing roof and the new fire-rated floor slab. In this way the void acts as a ca. 0.5–1 m deep "building services storey". With new floors constructed in timber, it must be ensured that the timber components in the void either feature fire-resistant cladding (see "Fire protection for timber facades", p. 19ff.) or the void is filled with non-combustible insulation (Fig. 2). Effective firefighting in this area is is either not possible or only to a limited extent, because the void is difficult or impossible to access.

Notes
[1] Dumler, Patrick; Engel, Thomas; Werther, Norman: Extra Hohe Häuser: HHX – Teilbericht Brandschutz zum Forschungsvorhaben "Extra Hohe Häuser". Hochschule München (funding organisation Zukunft Bau), 2021. https://mediatum.ub.tum.de/node?id=1648340
[2] ibid.

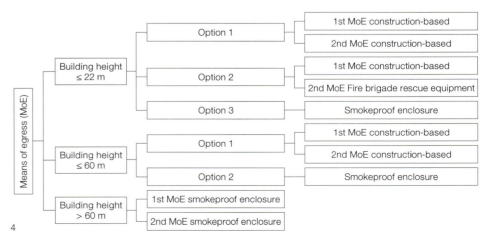

4

Roof Extension Construction

Manfred Stieglmeier

Building in existing stock by adding storeys requires not only consideration of architectural and regulatory aspects but also in-depth engagement with the construction requirements of the existing fabric, the reusability of the additional building components and their imposed pollutant load. The building survey and investigation of the existing construction elements take on considerable importance. This is not limited to the visual assessment of the architectural type and surroundings but also requires a thorough investigation of the construction components, e.g. by taking core samples for material testing, in order to obtain as much knowledge as possible about the existing fabric for the design of the fire protection, sound insulation and building services equipment. Particularly relevant are the reserves of load-carrying capacity of the foundations, walls, columns and ceilings. The latter can often only bear a small amount of additional load because, as the top enclosure element, they were usually designed for use as roofs and not as floors. In these cases, further structural measures are necessary to increase the load-carrying capacity of the existing construction, improve sound insulation and enhance the building's stiffness. In timber construction there are several approaches to providing a solution (Fig. 2) [1]:
- Increasing the shear stiffness of the original floor e.g. connecting wood based material panels with screws, creating a timber concrete composite ceiling
- Strengthening the effective structural cross section (e.g. attaching a further beam layer or cross-laminated timber panels)
- Replacement of the existing construction with a new timber floor

As an alternative to transferring loads via the floor of the top storey, loads can be supported by the existing walls and columns. Lightweight timber constructions consisting of large-format timber panel elements or floors and roofs comprising hollow box elements allow larger spans to be bridged between external walls or structural internal walls with load-bearing reserves. There are three different approaches to achieving load transfer:
- Load transfer points coincide with those of the existing building
- Load transfer through an intermediate construction
- Load transfer through an independent load-bearing structure

When the load transfer points coincide with those of the existing building, the loads can be applied directly to the existing structural system. When load transfer takes place through an intermediate construction, the new construction is aligned crosswise to the existing structural system. This allows loads to be transferred through multiple storeys. Concentrating the load to be transferred in structural components inside the building offers greater freedom for the architectural design of the roof extension facades because they are free of load-bearing elements. In addition, it is also possible to support the loads from the construction and from the new use of the roof extension with an independent load-bearing structure and foundations. This type of construction is especially suitable for projects involving facade modernizations.

The low self-weight of timber construction is a considerable advantage compared to conventional forms of construction in mobilizing the load-bearing reserves of the existing building. Three-storey roof extensions, such as the Rauti-Huus project in Zurich, can only be realized if e.g. hollow box ceilings with slender columns minimize materials consumption and,

1   Added storeys and extension, Deutscher Alpenverein (DAV) headquarters, Munich (DE) 2021, ELEMENT A. Architekten, hiendl_schineis architektenpartnerschaft
   a Installation of the new floor construction comprising timber beams and precast concrete elements
   b Installation of the load-bearing structure for adding the atrium extension
2   Various floor retrofit options
   a Increasing the shear stiffness of the existing floor
   b Strengthening the effective structural cross section
   c Replacement of the existing construction with a new timber floor
3   Load transfer from the roof extension, various structural systems
   a Load-bearing external wall, roof extension follows the existing structural system
   b Skeleton frame, roof extension follows the existing structural system
   c Parallel shear wall construction, roof extension follows the existing structural system
   d Load-bearing external wall, roof extension as an independent structural system
   e Load-bearing external wall, roof extension supported by large-format wall elements arranged crosswise to the existing structural system
   f Load-bearing external wall, loads from the roof extension distributed by long-span beams arranged crosswise to the existing structural system

1a   b

thus, reduce the self-weight of the new structure (see "Vertical extension for flats in Zurich", p. 55f.). Prefabrication paves the way for rapid installation on site, reducing the risk of weather-related damages. After demolition of the existing roof construction, the topmost floor slab surface is exposed to weather impacts. This can potentially harm uses on the floors below. Therefore, it is worthwhile to integrate suitable protection measures, such as enclosures in the form of temporary tents or provisional foil coverings, as part of preparations for the project (Fig. 3).

Construction process

Knowledge of the existing conditions of a building both in terms of construction and required load-bearing reserves is a decisive necessity for the planning and design of a roof extension. The spatial plan and construction layout of a roof extension are determined by the building type, the circulation system, the way load-bearing walls and columns delineate interiors as well as by the position of the riser shafts for the existing building services infrastructure. The manner and method of construction of the roof extension depends largely on the construction-based details of the existing building. The following examples for construction-based approaches are oriented on principle illustrations (Fig 4, 5, p. 66f.) derived from the guidelines on roof extensions formulated in the Zukunft Bau study [2].

Create a suitable starting point
Prior to planning a roof extension, it is necessary to investigate the floor of the top storey in order to find a suitable structural starting point. After demolition of the existing roof, there are generally

two initial situations for this "foundation" for the rooftop extension (Fig. 4a, 5a, p. 66f.):
• Structural floor without parapet / knee wall
• Structural floor with parapet / knee wall supporting the roof extension construction

If the existing parapet is made from masonry, it is unsuitable for use as the base for the roof extension because it lacks stability for inserting anchor bolts

and needs to be demolished. In most cases, a reinforced concrete parapet can be reused in this way. An assessment must be made to ascertain the degree of reinforcement and the extent of work required to form a level bearing surface on the component. However, the reuse of the existing parapet quite often restricts the possibility of installing French windows flush with floors to provide barrier-free access to loggias or balconies. A roof extension typically involves a change of use of the existing attic. Therefore the

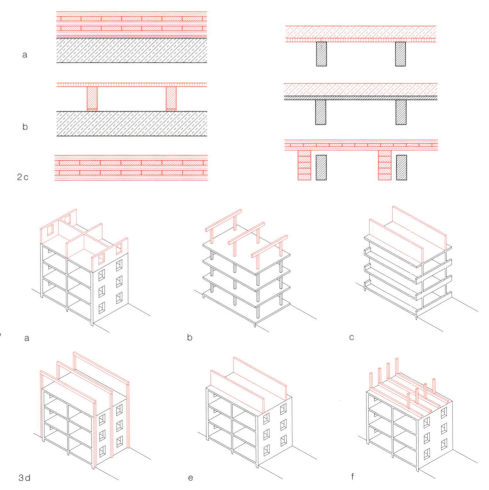

a   b   c

2c

3d   e   f

4,5 Construction process for a roof extension using
timber panel construction elements, sketches
showing principles
a Create a suitable structural starting point (the
demolished components are shown in yellow)
b Install components appropriate to the new
requirements and use
c Form the component joints between the roof
extension and the existing fabric

**Insulation of floor structure and roof extension
(no original parapet)**

**External wall modernization with prefabricated
elements and roof extension (parapet removed)**

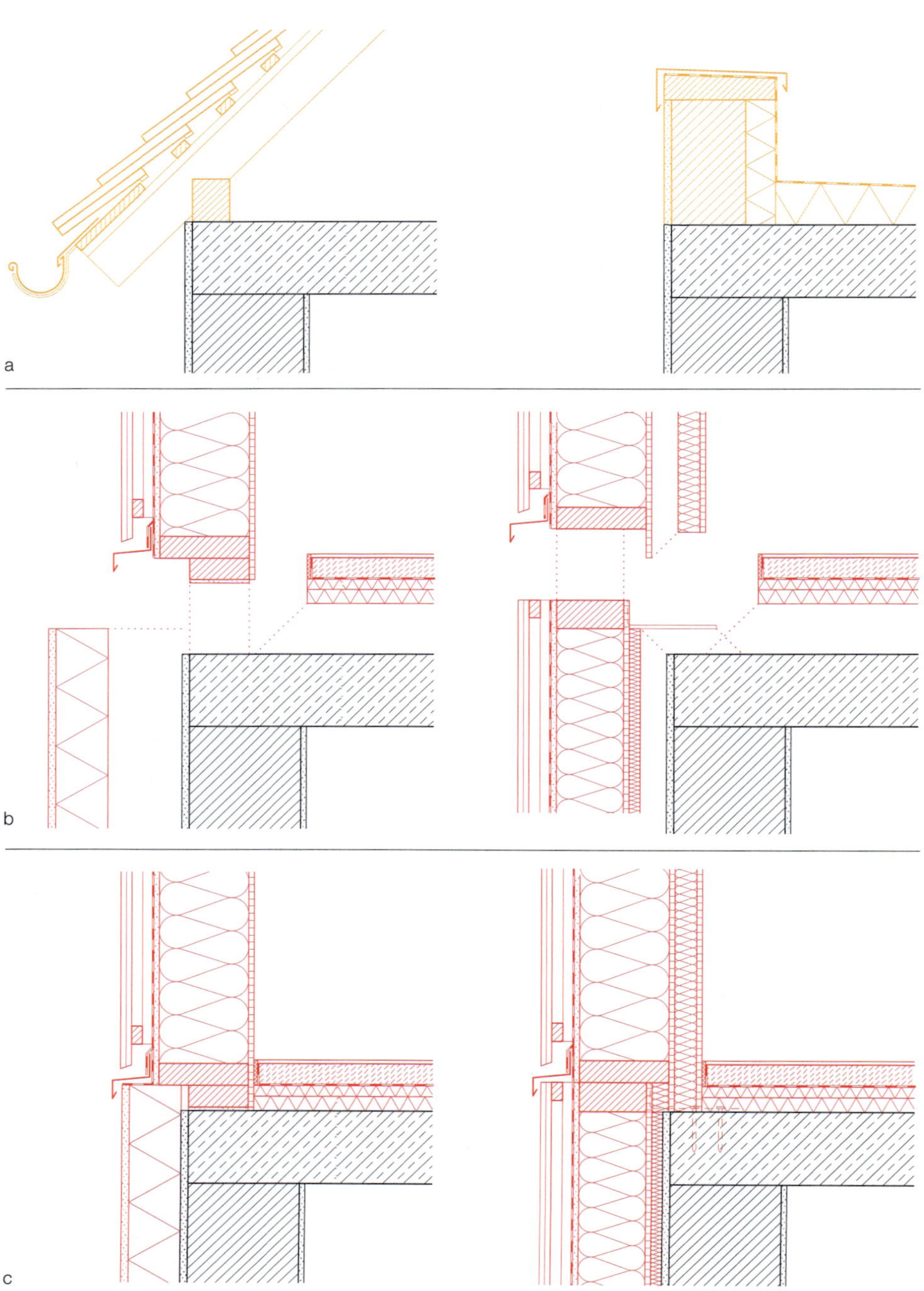

a

b

4 c

load-bearing capacity of the top floor
must be evaluated in order to ensure that
it can transmit the loads from the roof
extension. This may result in structural
measures to improve the load-bearing
capacity (Fig. 2, p. 65).

Type of construction and load distribution
If the top floor cannot be adequately
strengthened, then a new means of distributing the self-weight and live loads
from the roof extension, an additional
structural component, will be required.
The new level can, for instance, comprise
a grid structure or panel construction
combined with a beam layer. Loads are
transferred directly into the original walls
or columns of the existing building. The
new framework of beams, load-bearing
walls or wall-support beams distributing
the loads should be optimally designed to
transfer loads efficiently from the roof
extension into the load-bearing components of the existing building (Fig. 5).
Voids created between the floor of the
existing building and the new load-distrib-
uting construction can be used to install
building services etc. for the rooftop
extension. Lightweight partition walls can
be flexibly configured on the new
load-bearing construction, provided the
loads resulting from them have been
included in the dead loads from the roof
extension.

**Connection of the roof extension to the
existing fabric**

Concerning energy consumption, the
requirements applicable to a roof extension are the same as those for new construction. As a result, the new, modified
component is usually built to a higher
standard of energy efficiency. The connection details at the transition of the roof
extension to the existing building fabric

therefore require particularly careful consideration with respect to building physics (Fig. 4). If the intention is to not upgrade the energy-efficiency performance of the existing external walls, then cold bridges may be created at the transition between the old and the new construction. In order to avoid these, the external wall must be clad in insulation at least to some extent in the area of the transition. Architecturally and in terms of building physics, however, this approach is not a satisfactory solution in most cases. Therefore, a roof extension should ideally be designed and built at the same time as an energy-efficiency refurbishment of the existing external walls.

Roof extension with external wall modernization
In building physics and economic terms, it is worthwhile to combine a roof extension to a building with an energy-efficiency modernization of its external walls. Timber frame construction offers the opportunity to modernize the external walls and extend the roof at the same time. Prefabrication takes place as part of an extensive digital process chain, giving rise to synergies that result in rapid on-site installation times. The transition in the building envelope between the existing building fabric and the roof extension can receive a homogeneous visual character by embedding the slab edge of the existing building in the modernized wall construction. (Fig. 4, right column).

Sound insulation and services installations
There are no soundproofing requirements for the roof construction above the top floor of an existing building. The roof extension and the associated change of use of the former attic means that measures to improve sound insulation are required. Component layers such as floor screeds and impact soundproofing need to be added and offer the opportunity for

Insulation of existing structure and roof extension with a new load-bearing construction (with original parapet)

Insulation of existing structure and roof extension with a new load-bearing construction (original parapet / knee wall removed)

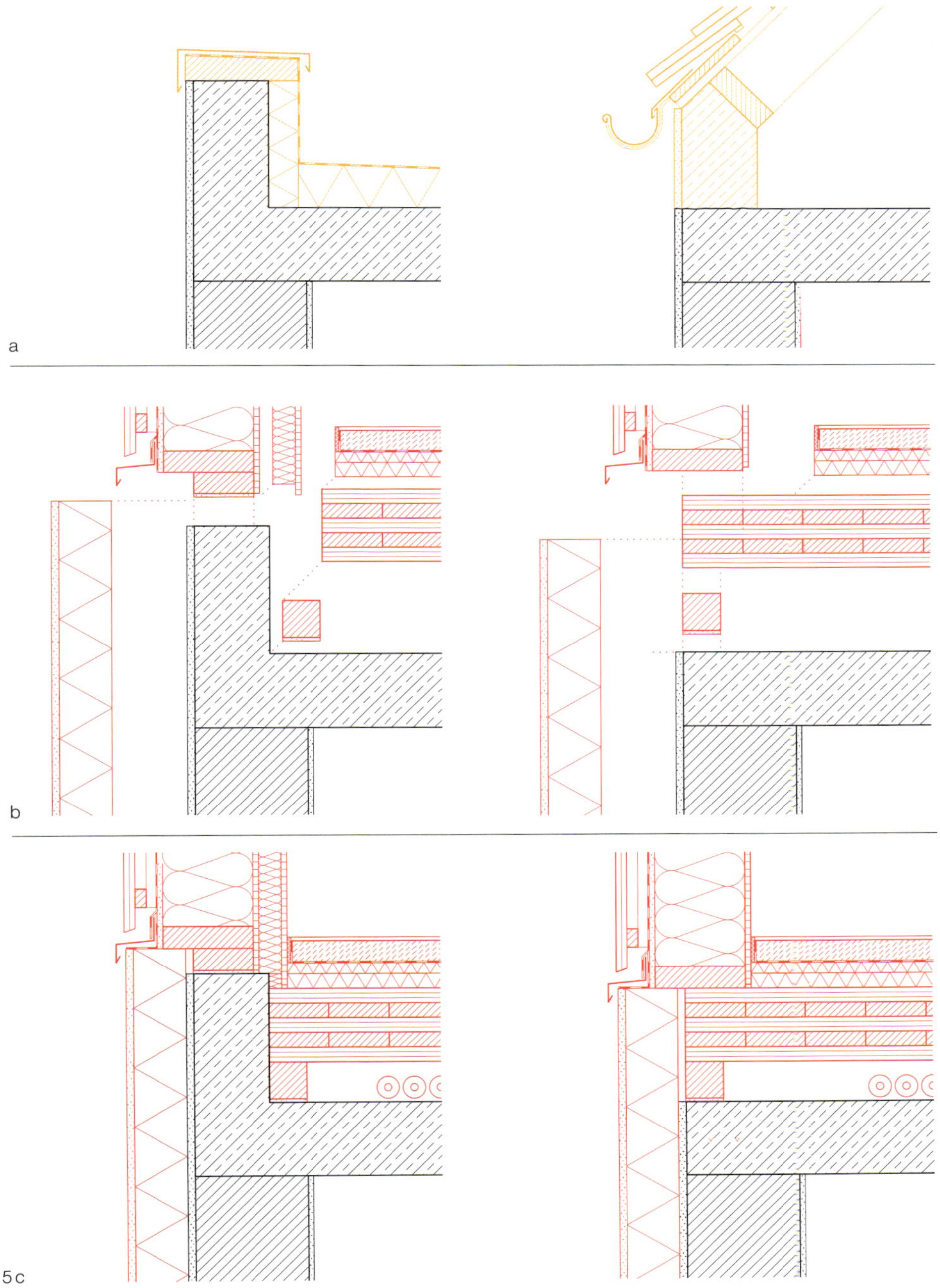

a

b

5 c

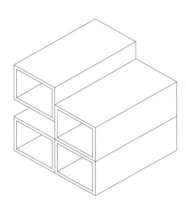
6

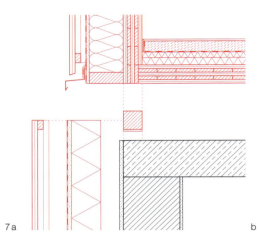
7 a

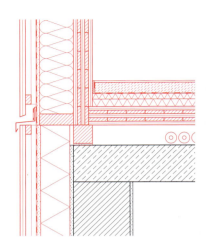
b

acoustic decoupling of the new layers, unlike the existing situation with the original roof (now floor) component (Fig. 4 b, c, 5 b, c, p. 66f.).
In addition to aspects of building physics and construction, the design of the roof extension must also take into account the building services pipework, ducts etc. at an early stage. The void between the existing roof and the new load-bearing construction offers space for the layout of building services. In some cases, disused flues or chimneys can serve as shafts inside the building to route services vertically. Alternatively, additional openings through the existing roof may be required or the building services can be housed in an external services shaft. This could be integrated into the wall construction as part of the refurbishment of the external wall (see "Building services", p. 44ff.).

Room modules

Roof extensions are preferably realized in timber not only because of the low component weight but particularly due to the short installation times on site enabled by the prefabrication of the building elements. The highest degree of prefabrication is offered by the room module system (Fig. 6). In most cases, the prefabricated rooms are manufactured with the surface finishes already in place along with the connections to attach neighbouring modules and their building services pipework, ducts etc. The time required for installation on site is reduced to the minimum as is the environmental impact on the area of the site and the disturbance to nearby residents caused by the building project. Room modules can be used to extend an existing building horizontally and vertically. The potentially long spans attainable with

vertical extensions and their high stiffness make them considerably more independent of the existing load-bearing structure. However, said structure, the circulation system and public utilities supply infrastructure of the existing building decisively influence meeting the spatial requirements. The existing ductwork and cable routes could ideally be extended. If this is not the case, it could be feasible to use the void between the original top storey roof and the floor of the room module to divert the services supply lines. The decision to use a room module system must be made early in the planning process because this form of construction has a considerable influence on the architectural design. One of the most important aspects to consider in relation to this approach are the transport distances between the timber construction contractor and the site. The dimensions of the

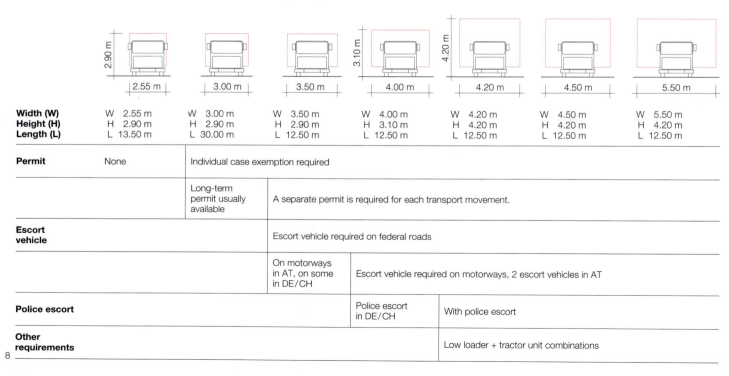

		2.55 m	3.00 m	3.50 m	4.00 m	4.20 m	4.50 m	5.50 m
Width (W)		W 2.55 m	W 3.00 m	W 3.50 m	W 4.00 m	W 4.20 m	W 4.50 m	W 5.50 m
Height (H)		H 2.90 m	H 2.90 m	H 2.90 m	H 3.10 m	H 4.20 m	H 4.20 m	H 4.20 m
Length (L)		L 13.50 m	L 30.00 m	L 12.50 m	L 12.50 m	L 12.50 m	L 12.50 m	L 12.50 m
Permit	None	Individual case exemption required						
		Long-term permit usually available	A separate permit is required for each transport movement.					
Escort vehicle		Escort vehicle required on federal roads						
			On motorways in AT, on some in DE/CH	Escort vehicle required on motorways, 2 escort vehicles in AT				
Police escort				Police escort in DE/CH	With police escort			
Other requirements					Low loader + tractor unit combinations			

8

68

6 Principle of load-transferring room modules
7 Roof extension with a room module above the top floor slab of the existing building, with concurrent external wall modernization
   a Installation of a room module
   b Component joints of a room module
8 Transport dimensions and the actions required for delivery to the installation site
9 Adding storeys and extension in timber construction, Deutscher Alpenverein (DAV) headquarters, Munich (DE) 2021, ELEMENT A. Architekten, hiendl_schineis architektenpartnerschaft
10 Deutscher Alpenverein (DAV) headquarters, Munich
   a Plan showing extensions (red), scale 1:750
   b Integration of the top floor slab into the new building envelope at the transition to the roof extension, vertical section scale 1:20

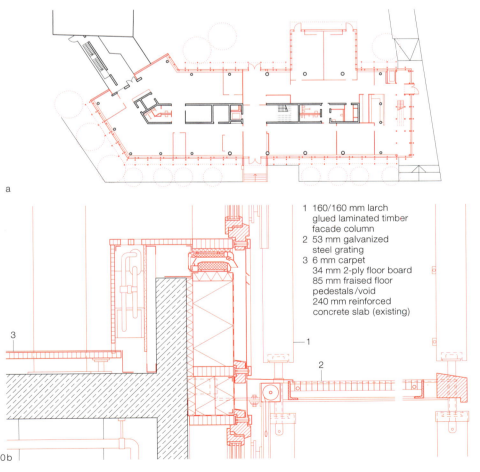

9

room modules are often limited by local features along the access route. A standard lorry can generally transport room modules with a length of about 13.50 m and a height of ca. 3.50 m (Fig. 8).

The design of a roof extension using room modules depends principally on the spatial concept and use. The width of modules is frequently the limiting factor in housing construction. Using them is sensible if the occupancy units are self-contained and repeated a number of times. Larger occupancy units can be made up of several room modules with open sides that can be joined together. Using room modules for roof extensions is frequently beneficial if the load-bearing structure and the use of the storeys below are different to those of the extension (Fig. 7).

DAV headquarters in Munich

The example of the new Munich branch office of the German Alpine Club (Deutscher Alpenverein, DAV) shows how the appearance of an existing building can change after receiving a new, homogeneous facade (Fig. 9). The 1970s-era building designed by Kurt Ackermann Architekten was gutted, leaving only the shell structure, and completely remodelled. The architects hiendl_schineis (competition and preliminary design) and Element A (final and detailed design) removed the concrete window parapets and added an atrium on the north side over the full height of the building. For reasons of weight, they chose to use timber hybrid construction for the two-storey rooftop addition. Roof extensions on skeleton frame buildings follow the same principle of load transfer as is the case in buildings with solid concrete or blockwork external walls. Ideally the loads are transferred directly into the existing building components, additional columns or shear walls.

In this case, however, the foundations required reinforcement. The timber-concrete composite slabs made from glued laminated timber beams with exposed concrete top layer were chosen to provide thermal storage mass. The glued laminated timber beams are placed on steel sections enveloped in 30 mm timber boards to provide fire protection. Similarly, for reasons of weight, the circulation core of the roof extension was also completed in solid timber. The facade consists of a post-and-beam construction in timber with ventilation elements in the window parapets to provide natural ventila-

tion (Fig. 10). The new building envelope was amended with a timber structure offset by 1.5 m on both lateral sides of the volume and featuring steel grating maintenance walkways and planting troughs for facade greening.

Notes
[1] Kaufmann, Hermann; Krötsch, Stefan; Winter, Stefan: Manual of Multi-Storey Timber Construction. Munich 2018, pp. 151–153
[2] Fath, Maren et al.: Leitlinie zur Vereinfachung der Planung und Durchführung von Aufstockungs- / Erweiterungsmaßnahmen als Nachverdichtungsmaßnahme in innerstädtischen Bereichen. Stuttgart 2019

a

1 160/160 mm larch glued laminated timber facade column
2 53 mm galvanized steel grating
3 6 mm carpet
   34 mm 2-ply floor board
   85 mm fraised floor pedestals/void
   240 mm reinforced concrete slab (existing)

10 b

Extensions

Manfred Stieglmeier

1548

1580

1620

1683

Bundesstiftung Baukultur, based on Julian Hanschke; Design: Heimann + Schwantes

1

Continued building in an existing context has always been the precondition for a respectful and economic way of dealing with traditional construction methods and available resources. This approach allows perpetuating the history of architecture and its context. In this manner, buildings can achieve a high degree of public acceptance throughout the ages – a prerequisite for sustainable construction. Buildings and cities are exposed to continual change as a result of innovations in building use requirements and new political or energy-related framework conditions. In earlier times, construction material was in short supply and expensive, but labour was relatively cheap. As a result, buildings were continually maintained and extended. Demolished buildings were regarded as stockpiles of building materials and therefore valuable stores of resources. Castles and palaces are examples of how buildings are further developed over time. Heidelberg Castle has been rebuilt, altered and extended continually since the 14th century, most recently by the addition of a restaurant in the former tack room (Fig. 1) [1]. Industrialization and the development of new construction techniques with modern materials, such as reinforced concrete, steel and glass, have led to the high efficiency and freedom characteristic of the building industry today and the disappearance of conversion culture. This was accompanied by the perception that specific modern requirements for a building are best satisfied with a tailor-made new construction and to achieve this through conversion would be too complicated. The function of a building was placed above its value and increasingly led to a demolition culture instead of continuously working on the existing building context. Today, embodied energy and existing conditions have been recognized by the public as valuable resources. As a result, the topic of continued building is once more in the focus of attention.

Extensions and implants

Modern timber construction is perfect for extending existing buildings because of its ability to be prefabricated in the workshop and rapidly installed on site. In this context, it is important to distinguish between extensions and implants.

Extensions

Most horizontal extensions are faced with a shortage of available land. In addition, the construction works for these extensions often have to be completed over a short time period and without interrupting everyday operation of a building. Precise planning focused on the specific situation from prefabrication to site logistics is essential to achieve this goal (see "Advantages of prefabrication", p. 54). There is a lack of guiding principles such as those previously identified for external wall modernizations (see p. 28ff.) or vertical extensions (see p. 49ff.). However, it is important that any building law issues raised by the changes to the existing volume and fabric are investigated (see "Public building law – legal framework", p. 56f.). An advantage of an extension is typically the way it enables connecting the new volume to the existing infrastructure (e.g. circulation, building services, outdoor areas, see "Ecological aspects". p. 51). Synergies arise when an extension involving adding storeys takes place at the same time as a facade refurbishment (see Deutscher Alpenverein (DAV) headquarters, Munich, p. 69).
The extension of the Bavarian State Office for the Environment (LfU) illustrates that particularly sensitive landscapes require an extremely low-emission ("soft") intervention (Fig. 2). The construction site, which was constricted by several trees deemed worthy of protection, demanded careful planning of the site logistics. The possibilities offered by prefabrication

1 Alterations and extensions at Heidelberg Castle between 1548–1683
2 Two-storey extension in timber, extension to the Bavarian State Office for the Environment (LfU), Wielenbach (DE) 2022, State Building Authority Weilheim, Stieglmeier Architekten/arcs architekten
3 Conversion of a residential and commercial building into student apartments, Ernas Haus, Dornbirn (AT) 2020, Ludescher + Lutz Architekten
   a Retention of a residential wing, addition of a stairwell and extension of the residential building, ground floor plan
   b Overhanging roof typical to the region and extension of loggias, cross section
   c Existing condition prior to intervention
   d Development of the existing context, creating a homogeneous ensemble

with timber and its material characteristics made it the preferred choice.

Implant – development inside existing stock
Easy-to-transport and dry building components are important for the continued use of existing buildings by installing what are often called implants inside the existing spatial structure. The integration of new functions into existing stock requires types of construction that can be realized without the use of cranes or lifting equipment or that make it possible to rationalize the building process (more efficient workflows, e.g. prefabricated elements) (see project example, p. 106ff.).

Transforming a residential and commercial building
In both an urban context as well as in rural areas, it is imperative to preserve the existing local identity and advance it in an adequate manner by dealing with the existing context respectfully. The Winderhof, a group of buildings in Oberdorf, Dornbirn dating back to 1890, was revitalized by densification and a new usage concept (Fig. 3). The settlement endured throughout the ages due to being safe from floods and the relatively good soil conditions. In 2016, a neighbouring residential building with an adjoining workshop was purchased and the ensemble created. The residential building was carefully gutted and refurbished while the former workshop, a barn, was taken down and replaced with a new solid wood construction. The basic structure of the former entire building was systematically utilized for the conversion, yet its function was altered. The existing elements and the new expansion merged, establishing a new architectural expression.
The Bregenz-based architects Ludescher + Lutz proposed a concept for the conversion aimed at further developing the

former residential building, demolishing the barn, and replacing it with a new volume to form a co-living ensemble with 18 housing units for students. The newly created basement contains additional space for bicycle storage and a laundry room. The deep roof overhangs typical to Rhine valley houses and the reversed gambrel roof of the barn were adapted as the characteristic element of the design and applied to these two buildings of the ensemble. The overhangs cover the entrance area and protect it against the weather. The building envelope comprised of of native silver fir connects the

old and the new, while the south side features a slat screen consisting of the same material to shield the loggias from intense sunlight. The retained masonry on the west facade was insulated externally before the vertical slat screens were installed, with each of the three storeys projecting 5 cm beyond the one below. The stairwell, an implant installed in the existing masonry, was constructed as a small independent structure also made of rough-sawn silver fir.

Notes
[1] Nagel, Reiner: Baukultur Bericht 2022/23 – Neue Umbaukultur. Bundesstiftung Baukultur. Berlin 2022

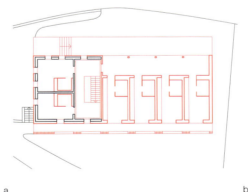

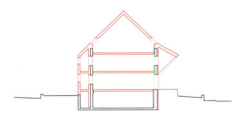

a

b

3 c

d

Exemplary projects

Unless otherwise indicated, all project information comes from the
listed architectural practices or other parties involved in the design.
Project texts: Cosima Frohnmaier, Stefan Krötsch

Residential and Commercial Building in Munich

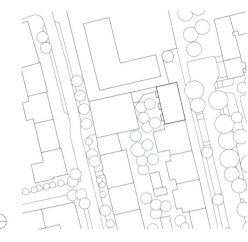

Architecture:	Braun Krötsch Architekten, Munich (DE)
Structural engineering:	Teuteberg Ingenieure, Baldham (DE)
Fire protection:	bauart – Beratende Ingenieure, Munich (DE)
Timber construction:	Zimmerei Anton Ambros, Hopferau (DE)

The residential and commercial building erected in 1972 in Munich's inner city was in urgent need of renovation: the windows did not meet current standards and the natural stone-clad curtain wall facade showed severe frost damage and needed to be removed. Following the energy-efficiency modernization of the envelope, the building side facing the street features a metal panel exterior. Depending on the individual viewpoint, the surface texture resembles fabric and appears to oscillate between light beige and athracite grey, between transparent and opaque.
In order to cause minimum disruption to the continuing use of the building and ensure the shortest possible construction time on site, the new building envelope comprises timber frame elements prefabricated in the workshop and measuring ca. 3 m × 13.5 m. Based on digital survey data, the elements were automatically and precisely manufactured to an accuracy of a few milimetres. The assembly of the six-storey facade took only days to complete so that any detrimental effects on the tenants and shop operators could be reduced to a minimum. Immediately after each pair of window bays was removed, a crane lifted each external wall element incorporating the already integrated new windows, pre-fitted slatted outdoor blind fittings and the expanded metal cladding into place. The timber frame construction is connected to the existing building structure by brackets. Drive-in beech dowels precisely connect one element to the next one, from bottom to top. A horizontal fire barrier is installed at every second floor level in the rear-ventilated cavity of the expanded metal exterior.
Inside the building, the window reveals are clad with prefabricated frames consisting of wood-based panels. Their installation was quick and dust-free. In follow, applying an interior render layer was not required.

Site plan
Scale 1:2500
Floor plan · section
Scale 1:400

1   Shops
2   Pharmacy
3   Entrance
4   Underground parking
    garage
5   One-room flat
6   Two-room flat
7   Three-room flat
8   Medical practice

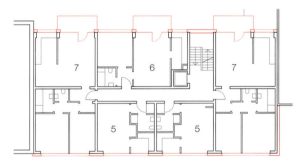

Sixth floor

Third floor

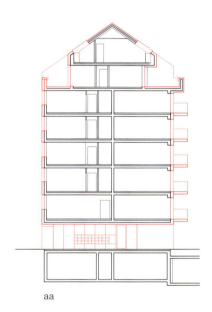

aa

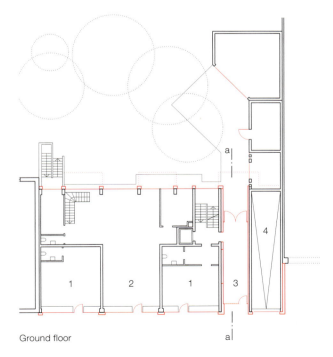

Ground floor

Simone Rosenberg

Isometric illustration, connection principle
Scale 1:20
Horizontal section · vertical section
Scale 1:20

1. 60/20 mm expanded metal anodized
   aluminium mesh
   80/30 mm aluminium Z-section framing
   facade membrane, breathable
   15 mm wood fibreboard
   60/180 mm structural timber (KVH) frame,
   180 mm cellulose fibre
   thermal insulation filling
   15 mm OSB board
   45 mm mineral wool compensation layer
   ca. 35 mm thermal insulation (existing)
   200 mm reinforced concrete (existing)
   15 mm render (existing)
2. 2 mm canted sheet aluminium
3. 25 mm wood-based panel window reveal frame
   continuous on 3 sides, coated
4. Window: triple glazing in timber-aluminium frame,
   $U = 1.0$ W/m²K
5. 40 mm concrete walkway paving
   35 mm gravel bedding
   40 mm drainage mat
   5 mm nonwoven fabric
   synthetic roof waterproofing membrane
   120 mm PUR thermal insulation
   bituminous vapour barrier, primer
   250 mm reinforced concrete slab (existing)
   15 mm render
6. 10/40 mm RHS flat steel railing, hot-dipped
   galvanized powder-coated
7. 2 mm aluminium sheet parapet coping
8. 50 mm beech dowel
9. Exterior slat blind sun protection
10. 25 mm coated wood-based panel interior
    window sill

Braun Krötsch Architekten

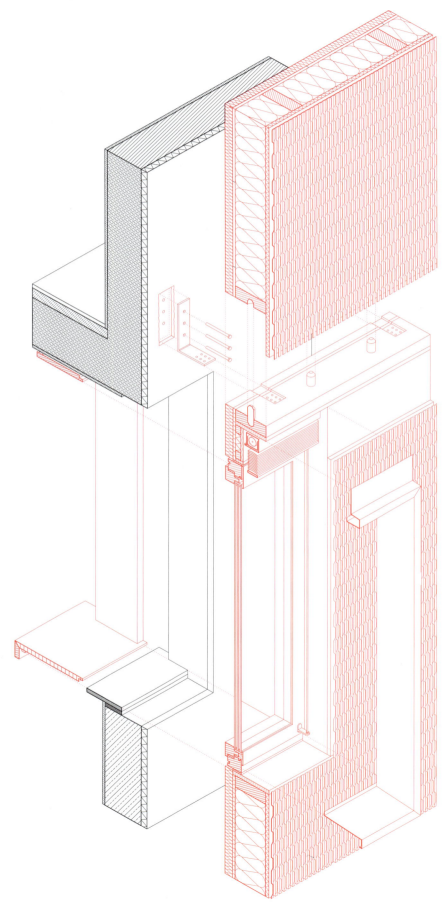

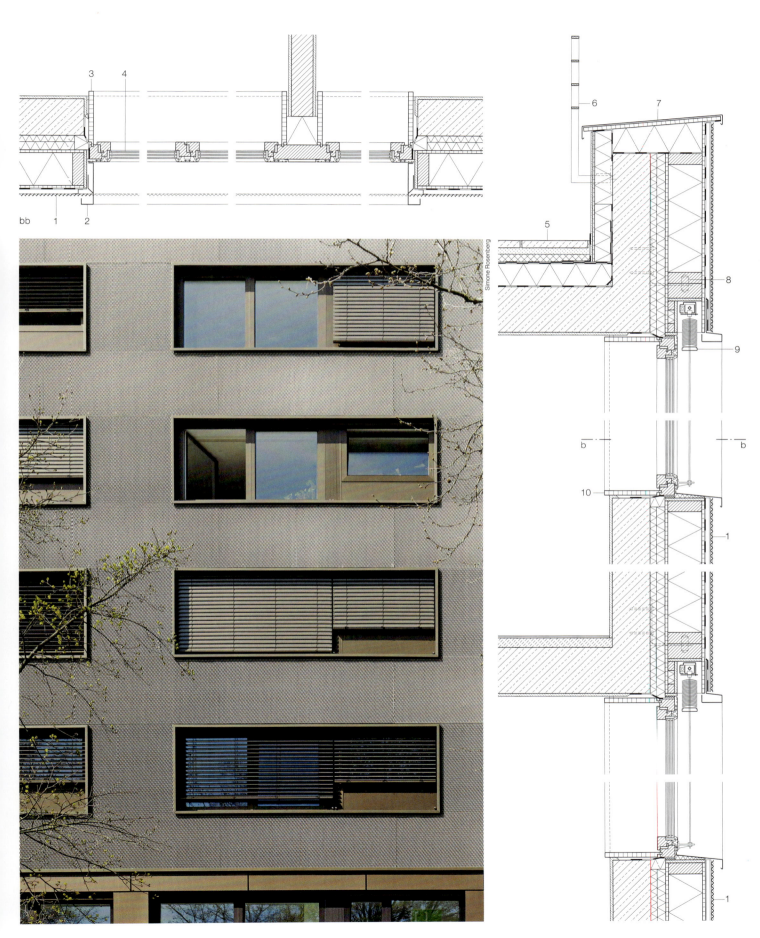

bb 1 2

3 4

5 6 7 8 9 10 1

b b

1

Simone Rosenberg

Single Family House in Hittisau

Architecture:	Georg Bechter Architektur + Design, Hittisau (AT)
Client:	Martina and Christoph Gell, Hittisau (AT)
Structural engineering:	planDREI Hammerer, Andelsbuch (AT)
Site management:	Bischof & Zündel, Lingenau (AT)
Building physics:	Erich Reiner Ingenieurbüro für Holzwirtschaft und Bauphysik, Bezau (AT)

The 1960s residential building featured a roof that projected beyond the walls and was slightly L-shaped in plan. The masonry brick structure lacked insulation and therefore difficult to heat. After initial deliberations on demolishing the building, the clients were convinced by the idea to renovate it.

The spatial structure of the building is defined by a load-bearing central wall, with the living and bedrooms facing south on the lower side of the sloping site and the auxiliary rooms facing north. As part of the conversion, the internal stairs were moved from east to west so that the outdoor steps lead into the internal circulation system. This enables dividing the two residential storeys into independent units at any time in the future. The area where the stairs formerly entered now serves as an open space with a tall ceiling above the living and cooking areas and creates new, open spatial relationships within the building. The new facade comprises a frame with solid timber studs and beams. It is arranged in front of the existing masonry wall, while the space in-between is filled with a 24 cm thick layer of wood fibre insulation. Spruce shingle cladding attached to wood sheathing is set in front of the insulation layer, thereby maintaining a rear ventilation cavity. The new windows with their wood frames were installed in the insulation layer in front of the existing external wall, thus omitting any cold bridges. They are protected by a *Wurf,* a projecting element consisting of shingles above the windows that are angled outward, as well as protruding reveals and sills.

The roof trusses were replaced and insulated for structural reasons and to enable the installation of photovoltaic panels. New impact soundproofing screed was added to improve the sound insulation of the brick floors above the basement and ground floor rooms and to incorporate underfloor heating.

Georg Bechter Architektur + Design

Georg Bechter Architektur + Design

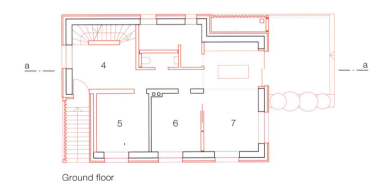

aa

Site plan
Scale 1:2000
Section · floor plans
Scale 1:250

1   Garage
2   Basement
3   Storage room
4   Cloakroom
5   Office
6   Living space
7   Cooking/eating space
8   Children's rooms
9   Parents' bedroom
10 Void
11 Attic

Ground floor

Attic

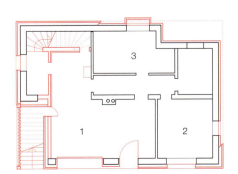

Basement

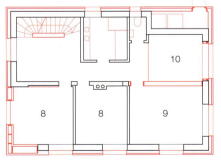

First floor

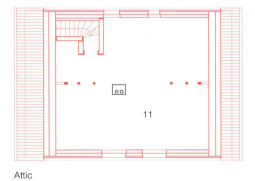

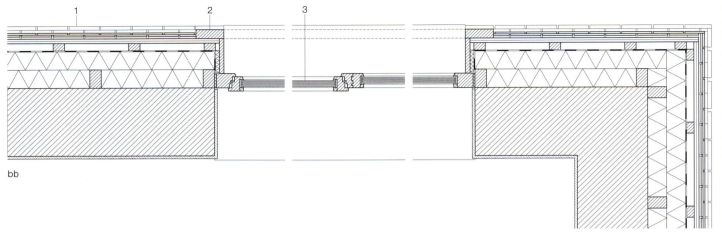

bb

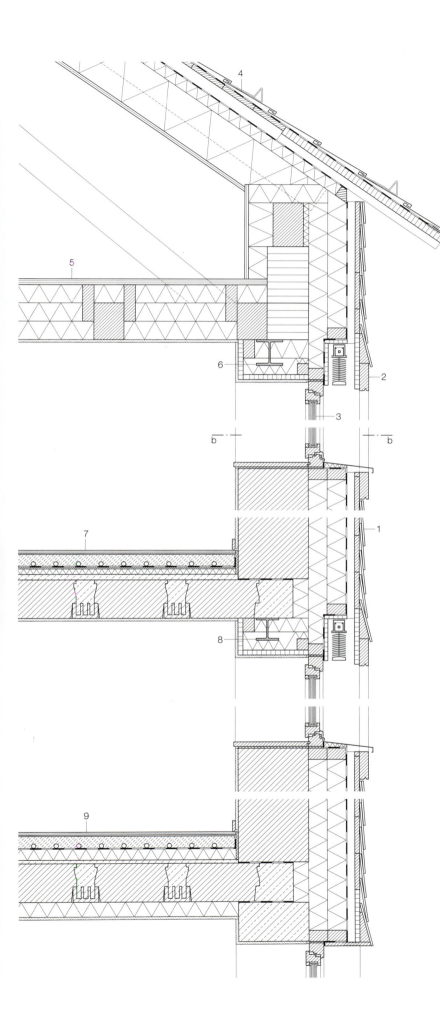

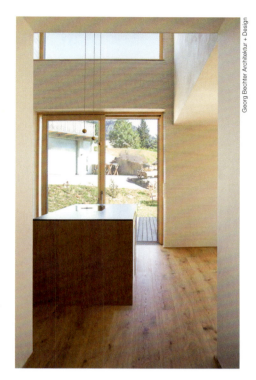

Georg Bechter Architektur + Design

Horizontal section · vertical section
Scale 1:20

1   25 mm triple layer spruce split shingle cladding
    25 mm timber sheathing
    40 mm battens / rear ventilation
    wind barrier
    2× 100 mm thermal insulation
    400 mm masonry (existing)
    15 mm clay render
2   50/150 mm continuous timber frame, spruce
3   Window: triple glazing in spruce frame
4   2 mm aluminium roof shingles
    bituminous waterproofing membrane
    27 mm timber sheathing
    60 mm battens / rear ventilation
    breathable underlay
    60 mm rigid wood fibre panel
    140/240 mm rafters
    240 mm insulation between rafters
    30 mm structural timber
5   30 mm timber floorboards
    60/200 mm levelling battens in combination with
    160/200 mm floor beams (existing)
    wood fibre insulation between
    15 mm gypsum board
6   140 mm wide flange steel beam
7   Top floor construction:
    15 mm oak parquet
    65 mm heating screed
    PE foil
    10 mm impact soundproofing
    30 mm installation layer / EPS insulation
    240 mm brick floor (existing)
    15 mm render
8   120 mm wide flange steel beam
9   Ground floor construction:
    15 mm oak parquet
    65 mm heating screed
    vapour barrier
    60 mm impact soundproofing
    240 mm brick floor (existing)
    80 mm EPS thermal insulation
    15 mm render

Primary School in Neuruppin

Architecture: CKRS Architekten, Berlin (DE)
Client: Fontanestadt Neuruppin (DE)
Structural engineering: ifb frohloff staffa kühl ecker, Berlin (DE)
Landscape architecture: Hradil Landschaftsarchitektur, Neuruppin (DE)
Timber construction: Treskower Zimmerer und Dachdecker, Märkisch Linden (DE)

The Wilhelm-Gentz Primary School in Neuruppin, about 70 kilometres north-west of Berlin, was built in 1972. It no longer met current needs nor the future expectations of a sustainable primary school. Lack of capacity and increased requirements in relation to thermal insulation and fire protection called for an extension and refurbishment.

CKRS Architekten emerged as the winners of an architectural competition in 2018. They succeeded in redesigning the former "Erfurt" type precast slab structure into a modern school building receiving ample daylight. The ensemble is composed of three volumes: the redesigned former precast panel system building, the L-shaped extension and the new sports hall. A new, generously dimensioned main entrance connects the existing block to the extension, serves as a central meeting point and provides exhibition space.

As part of the refurbishment, the non-structural external walls of the existing building were taken down. On the north side of the existing building, the architects added a new, up to 3.90 m wide play corridor as part of the circulation system with spacious access areas at the stairwells. This reinforced concrete structure connects seamlessly to the existing and provides longitudinal stiffness. The basic reinforced concrete structure of the similarly built extension consists of solid floor slabs, pilasters and columns. In order to visually connect new and old, all building parts received an envelope consisting of prefabricated timber frame wall elements complete with thermal insulation covered with larch siding. Thus, the facade elements serve purposes of thermal protection and visible enclosure. The interior face and the floor slab edge detail ensure fire protection as well as soundproofing between floors.

Continuous horizontal sheet steel fire stops in the area of the window parapets prevent fire from spreading in the rear-ventilation cavity and across the facade surface.

Stefan Josef Müller

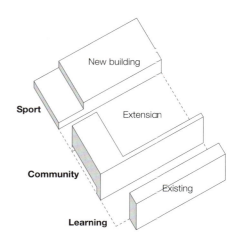

Site plan
Scale 1:2500
Sections · floor plans
Scale 1:750

1 Foyer / assembly hall
2 Teachers'/children's kitchenette
3 Classroom
4 Group room
  Multipurpose room
5 Entrance / reception
6 Group room
  Design
7 Handicrafts
8 Equipment room
9 Multipurpose hall
10 Changing room
11 IT room
12 Classroom
13 Group room
  Experience zone
14 Store
15 Group room
  Multimedia

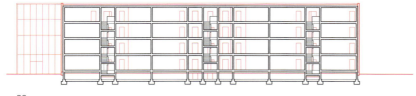

aa

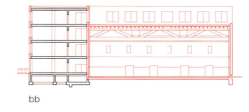

bb

Third floor

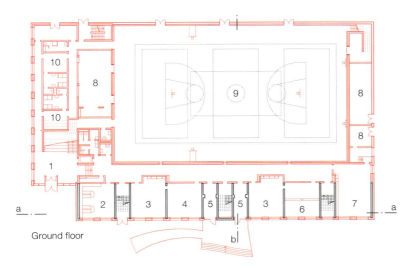

Ground floor

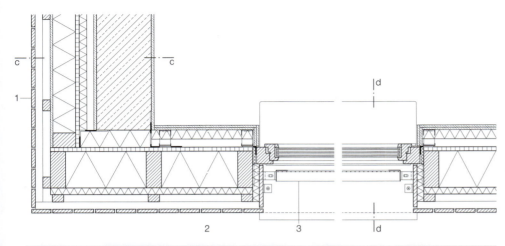

Horizontal section • vertical sections
Scale 1:20

1   20/100 mm larch sheathing, rough-sawn
    40/60 mm battens
    40/60 mm counter battens
    15 mm gypsum board, breathable
    80/120 mm structural timber (KVH) studs
    120 mm wood fibre insulation in the
    panels between
    22 mm OSB
    40 mm mineral wool compensation insulation,
    non-combustible (> 1000 °C)
    15 mm min. construction gap
    15 mm render (existing)
    290 mm lightweight concrete wall (existing)
    15 mm render
2   20/100 mm larch sheathing, rough-sawn
    40/60 mm battens
    40/60 mm counter battens
    35 mm wood fibreboard
    80/200 mm structural timber (KVH) studs
    200 mm wood fibre insulation in panels between
    22 mm wood-based panel, glued airtight
    45 mm construction gap
    50 mm building services cavity / insulation
    25 mm 2-ply gypsum board
3   40/40 mm steel angle frame fall protection,
    galvanized, powder-coated
    expanded metal filling panels, spot-welded
    to the frame
4   Triple glazing in wood frame, U = 1.00 W/m²K
5   8–10 mm 2-ply bituminous roof membrane,
    waterproof
    20 cm average depth EPS insulation,
    min. 2 % falls
    4 mm vapour barrier
    70 mm average depth screed, falls (existing)
    250 mm brick-concrete composite slab (existing)
    Acoustic ceiling:
    35 mm wood wool lightweight board, attached
    directly by 125 mm hanger
    60 mm mineral wool rear filling
6   Sheet titanium-zinc parapet coping
7   25 mm linoleum, glued
    65 mm cementitious screed
    1 mm PE foil separating layer
    20 mm footfall impact soundproofing
    40 mm average depth cement-bound
    levelling layer
    250 mm brick-concrete composite slab (existing)
    Acoustic ceiling:
    35 mm wood wool lightweight panel, attached
    directly by 125 mm hanger
    60 mm mineral wool rear filling
8   30 mm oak window sill
9   12 mm fibre-cement plinth protection panel

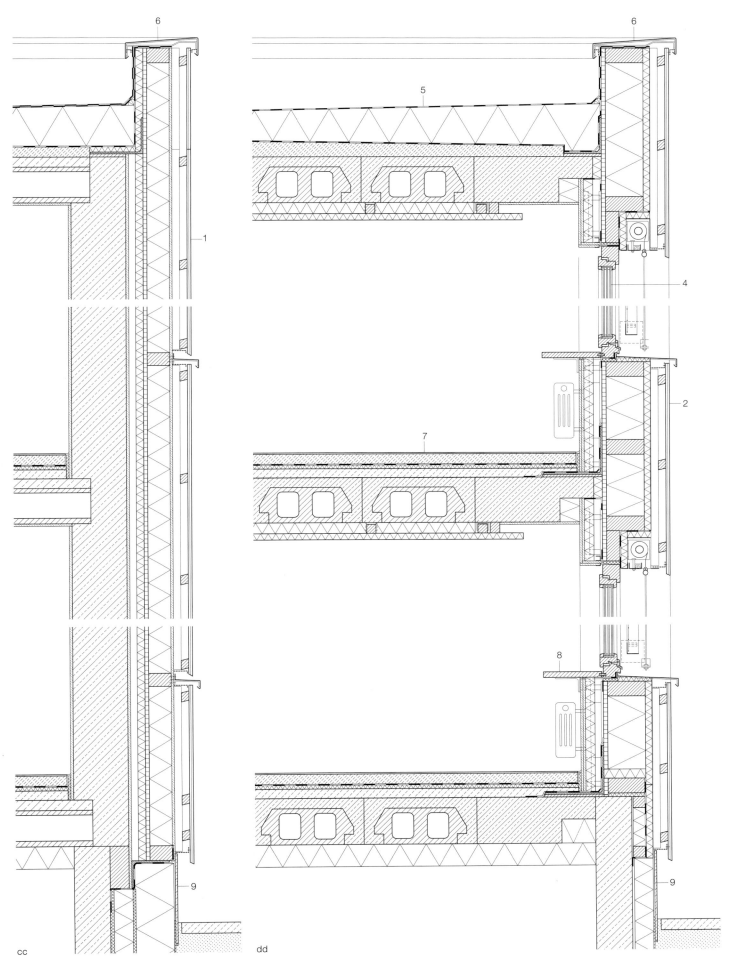

cc

dd

Town House in Linz

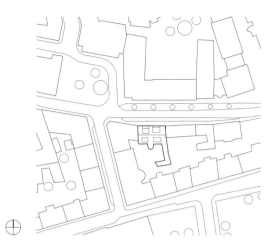

Architecture:	mia2 Architektur, Linz (AT)
Client:	Sandra Gnigler and Gunar Wilhelm, Linz (AT)
Structural engineering:	Kotlaba, Thalheim bei Wels (AT)
Contractor:	Simader Baumeister und Zimmermeister, Linz (AT)

In most cases, dilapidated buildings on inner-city sites that are not historically listed are demolished and replaced with new construction. Mia2 Architeken had acquired a townhouse in Linz for their own office and followed a different approach. Multiple construction phases led to a two-storey rooftop timber extension housing ten new apartments. The volume also contains atmospheric spaces for the architecture office, situated on the ground floor and covered by vaulted ceilings.

The first works on site involved strengthening the existing foundations, drying out the damp masonry with heating cables installed in the foundation area and demolishing the old floor slab. The architects used the soil beneath the slab as a clay pit to create prefabricated wall elements made of rammed earth, which were used to form a load-bearing wall under the ridge purlin in the second phase of the works. In the above-ground storeys, the original timber floors were retrofit with a top layer of concrete to form a timber-concrete composite slab. The existing gable roof was removed and replaced by a two-and-a-half-storey roof extension with a new gable roof, large glazed dormers and metal sheet cladding. Three angular steel frames span a column-free attic. For fire protection reasons, a non-combustible insulation layer, which would subsequently lie behind the timber cladding, was attached to the outer face of the timber frame walls, while the inner face of the wall was lined with gypsum board. The horizontal beams in the facade function as fire stops.

In the courtyard, a spiral staircase featuring specifically developed precast concrete elements replaces the steep original stairs inside the building. The flats are compact but include communicative balconies facing the planted internal courtyard.

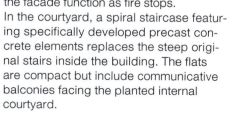

mia 2 Architektur

Site plan
Scale 1:2500
Floor plans · section
Scale 1:500

1 Entrance to flats
2 Entrance to
architecture office
3 Architecture office
4 Apartment
5 Garden courtyard
6 Cycle storage
7 Balcony
8 Maisonette
9 Void

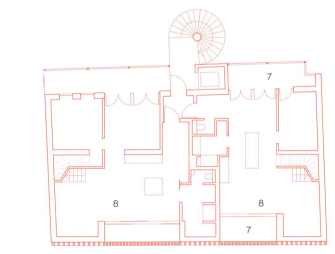

Fourth floor

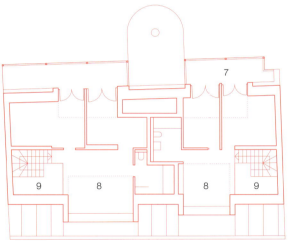

Fifth floor

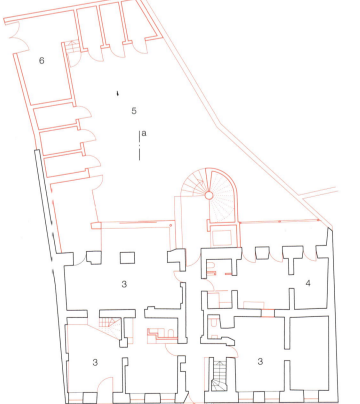

Ground floor

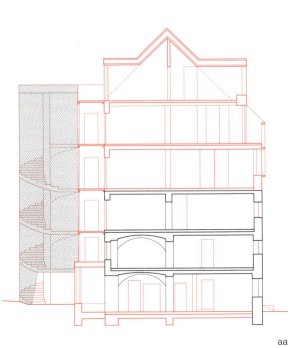

aa

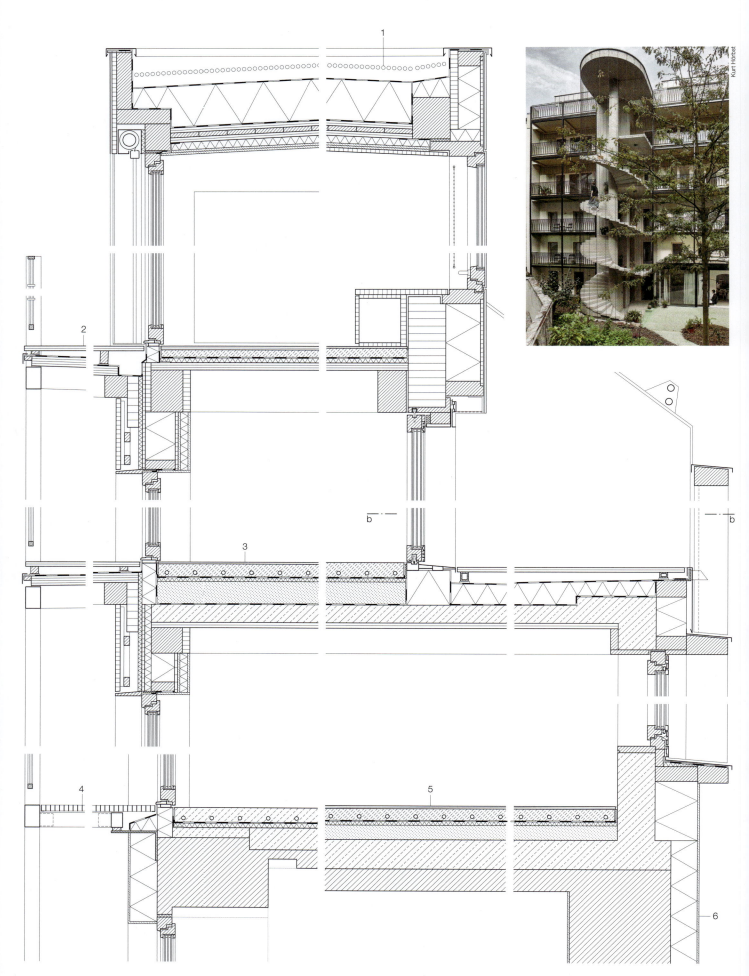

1

2

3

b

b

4

5

6

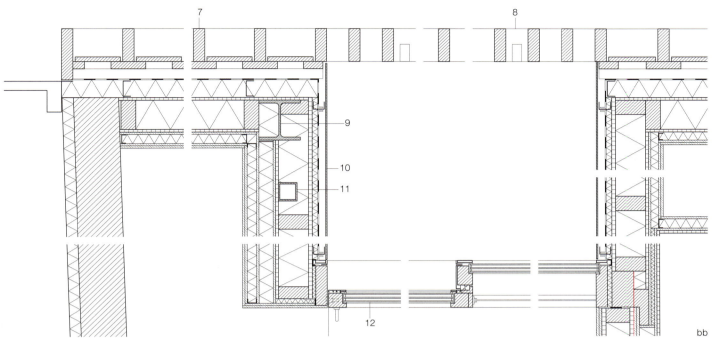

bb

Vertical section · horizontal section
Scale 1:20

1   80 mm gravel, 0.3 mm foil,
    220 mm EPS thermal insulation
    aluminium lined vapour barrier
    80 mm cross-laminated timber
    40 mm battens with mineral wool fill
    2× 12.5 mm gypsum board
    20 mm three ply spruce panel
2   24 mm timber lattice, battens, seal
    52 mm sheathing on 80/80 mm timber fire stop
    and 120/80 mm steel RHS
3   Linoleum 10 mm
    70 mm heating screed, PE foil
    20 mm impact soundproofing
    130 mm insulating fill, PE foil
    timber-concrete composite slab:
    100 mm reinforced concrete, 30 mm formwork
    140 mm timber beam ceiling
4   30/30 mm glassfibre reinforced plastic grating
5   15 mm wood flooring
    65 mm sanded heating screed, PE foil
    20 mm impact soundproofing, 90 mm insulating fill
    180 mm top concrete layer
    50–300 mm brick vault (existing)
6   20 mm render, 140 mm mineral foam
    300 mm masonry (existing)
    10 mm render, white
7   180/100 mm vertical timber slats
    (between horizontal fire stops)
    25 mm timber siding, 40 mm timber siding
    50/60 mm battens, wind barrier
    100 mm aluminium channels
    100 mm mineral wool insulation between
    16 mm DHF board
    160/80 mm wood blocking
    160 mm mineral wool thermal insulation between
    15 mm OSB board glued airtight
    12.5 mm gypsum board
    50 mm aluminium channels
    50 mm mineral wool thermal insulation between
    2× 12.5 mm gypsum board
8   180/100 mm timber parapet cap
9   220 mm wide flange steel column
10 4 mm aluminium composite panel,
    40 mm rear ventilation, wind barrier
    30 mm mineral wool; 16 mm resin-bonded medium
    density wood fibre panel, 80/160 mm wood blocking
    160 mm mineral wool thermal insulation between
    15 mm OSB glued airtight
    12.5 mm gypsum board
    50 mm aluminium channels
    50 mm mineral wool thermal insulation between
    2× 12.5 mm gypsum board
11 100/100 mm steel SHS bracing
12 Triple glazing in wood frame

Kurt Hörbst

Higher Technical College of Construction and Design in Innsbruck

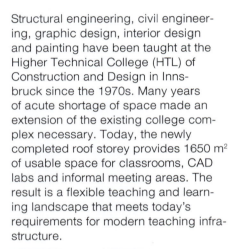

Architecture: ao-architekten, Innsbruck (AT)
Client: BIG – Bundesimmobiliengesellschaft, Vienna (AT)
Structural engineering: Alfred R. Brunnsteiner, Natters (AT)
Building physics: Fiby, Innsbruck (AT)
Building services: Bopp Ingenieure, Wörgl (AT)

Structural engineering, civil engineering, graphic design, interior design and painting have been taught at the Higher Technical College (HTL) of Construction and Design in Innsbruck since the 1970s. Many years of acute shortage of space made an extension of the existing college complex necessary. Today, the newly completed roof storey provides 1650 m² of usable space for classrooms, CAD labs and informal meeting areas. The result is a flexible teaching and learning landscape that meets today's requirements for modern teaching infrastructure.

Twenty-six northwest-facing roof skylights extend across the entire roof area of the four-storey existing building. The skylights allow daylight to permeate the interiors of the 26 m deep building and create a pleasant working atmosphere. The saw-toothed roof structure and the slate roofing in light grey hues are not obviously discernible from the outside. Circumferential black metal cladding encloses a 71 m long box that is seemingly elevated above the existing structure by a continuous strip window. The new roof extension is largely a timber structure. The solid cross-laminated timber walls are aligned with the facades and the glazed partitions

bordering the central zone at intervals of 5 m or 7.5 m and supported by steel brackets set on top of hollow steel sections measuring 140 mm by 140 mm. The shed roof structure is braced partly by steel trusses integrated into the construction replacing the otherwise used glue laminated timber beams. The trusses rest on the exposed bush-hammered concrete walls of the sanitary rooms, which also serve to stiffen the building. This allowed having a continuous horizontal band of sun protection glazing bordering the new rooms, offering a 360-degree panorama view of Innsbruck and the surrounding mountains.

David Schreyer

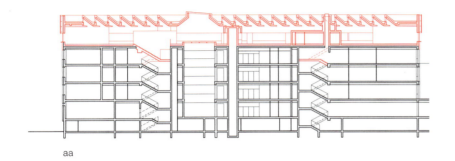

aa

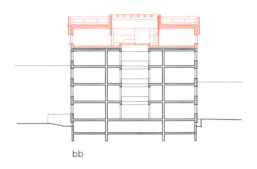

bb

Fourth floor

Site plan	7 Assembly hall
Scale 1:5000	8 Janitor's flat
Sections • floor plans	9 Library
Scale 1:750	10 Cafeteria
	11 Kitchen
1 Main building	12 Hall
2 Workshops	13 Open learning
3 Entrance	14 Structural glass
4 Janitor	floor above light well
5 Classroom	15 CAD lab
6 Light well	16 Terrace

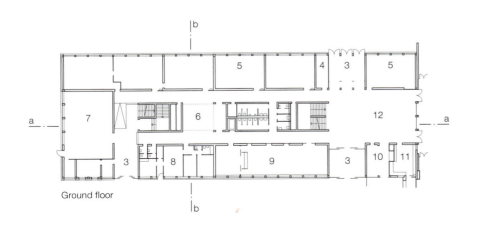

Ground floor

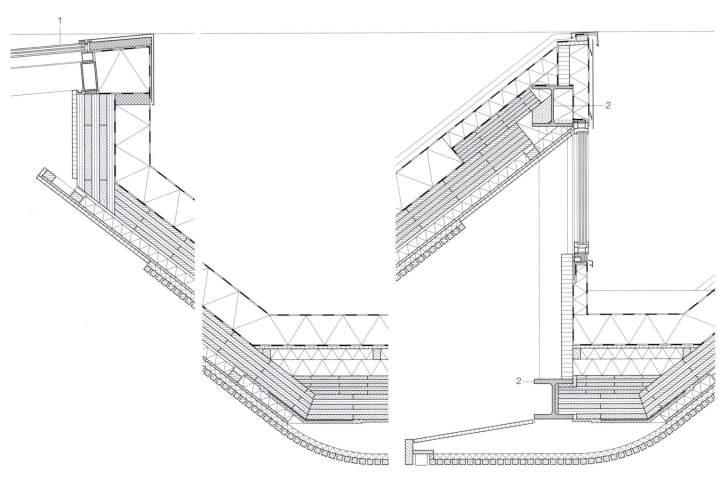

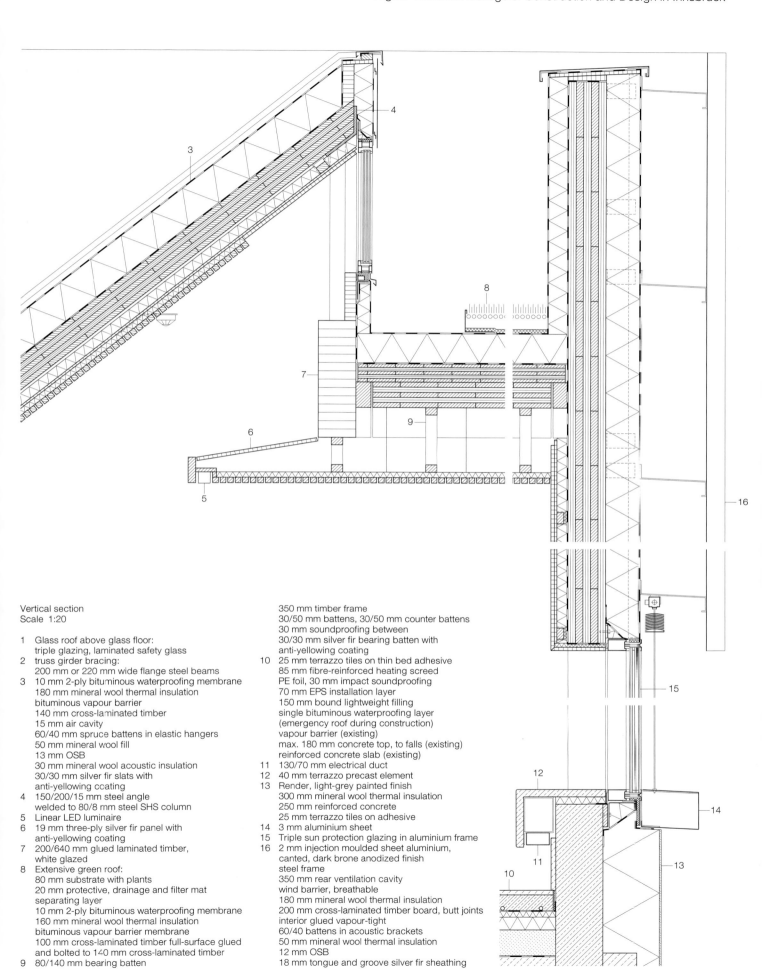

Vertical section
Scale 1:20

1 Glass roof above glass floor:
   triple glazing, laminated safety glass
2 truss girder bracing:
   200 mm or 220 mm wide flange steel beams
3 10 mm 2-ply bituminous waterproofing membrane
   180 mm mineral wool thermal insulation
   bituminous vapour barrier
   140 mm cross-laminated timber
   15 mm air cavity
   60/40 mm spruce battens in elastic hangers
   50 mm mineral wool fill
   13 mm OSB
   30 mm mineral wool acoustic insulation
   30/30 mm silver fir slats with
   anti-yellowing coating
4 150/200/15 mm steel angle
   welded to 80/8 mm steel SHS column
5 Linear LED luminaire
6 19 mm three-ply silver fir panel with
   anti-yellowing coating
7 200/640 mm glued laminated timber,
   white glazed
8 Extensive green roof:
   80 mm substrate with plants
   20 mm protective, drainage and filter mat
   separating layer
   10 mm 2-ply bituminous waterproofing membrane
   160 mm mineral wool thermal insulation
   bituminous vapour barrier membrane
   100 mm cross-laminated timber full-surface glued
   and bolted to 140 mm cross-laminated timber
9 80/140 mm bearing batten

350 mm timber frame
30/50 mm battens, 30/50 mm counter battens
30 mm soundproofing between
30/30 mm silver fir bearing batten with
anti-yellowing coating
10 25 mm terrazzo tiles on thin bed adhesive
   85 mm fibre-reinforced heating screed
   PE foil, 30 mm impact soundproofing
   70 mm EPS installation layer
   150 mm bound lightweight filling
   single bituminous waterproofing layer
   (emergency roof during construction)
   vapour barrier (existing)
   max. 180 mm concrete top, to falls (existing)
   reinforced concrete slab (existing)
11 130/70 mm electrical duct
12 40 mm terrazzo precast element
13 Render, light-grey painted finish
   300 mm mineral wool thermal insulation
   250 mm reinforced concrete
   25 mm terrazzo tiles on adhesive
14 3 mm aluminium sheet
15 Triple sun protection glazing in aluminium frame
16 2 mm injection moulded sheet aluminium,
   canted, dark brone anodized finish
   steel frame
   350 mm rear ventilation cavity
   wind barrier, breathable
   180 mm mineral wool thermal insulation
   200 mm cross-laminated timber board, butt joints
   interior glued vapour-tight
   60/40 battens in acoustic brackets
   50 mm mineral wool thermal insulation
   12 mm OSB
   18 mm tongue and groove silver fir sheathing

Conference Hotel in Salzburg

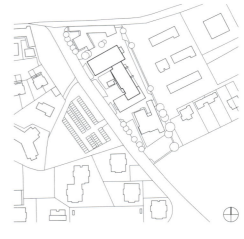

Architecture: sps architekten, Thalgau (AT)
Client: Kammer für Land- und Forst-
                      wirtschaft, Salzburg (AT)
Structural engineering: Ingenieurbüro Baueregger,
                      Salzburg (AT)
Timber construction: INNOVAHOLZ,
                      Niedernfritz (AT)

The Heffterhof Hotel in Salzburg is used mostly as a conference and seminar centre. The northern block of the H-shaped building complex was extended by one storey comprised of timber room modules. The hotel features a total of 14 new barrier-free double rooms consisting of lobby, sitting and sleeping areas, bathroom and loggia. The modules face north-west or south-east and are accessed by a central corridor with overhead skylights to allow daylight to enter. The additional auxiliary rooms are situated near the connection to the central block.

Because the hotel operates all year round, it was essential to find a system that would allow the roof extension to be completed within seven weeks, a timeframe determined by the operator. The solution entailed delivering prefabricated room modules on site complete with finished floors, tile surfaces and doors and merely stacking them on top of each other. All that remained to do on site was to mount the balconies, install the services connections in the hall area and attach the cladding to the corridor walls. The roof extension follows the structural grid of the existing hotel rooms

below so that load transmission was direct and sanitary services required no diversions. The 4.80 × 6.50 m modules are constructed from cross-laminated timber and supported on elastomeric bearings resting on the existing structure. The double walls and floors are insulated from one another and from the existing structure to prevent the transmission of structure-borne sound and benefit from the characteristics of room module prefabrication to optimize soundproofing. The timber construction is visible in the interior and lends the new rooms a warm, friendly atmosphere.

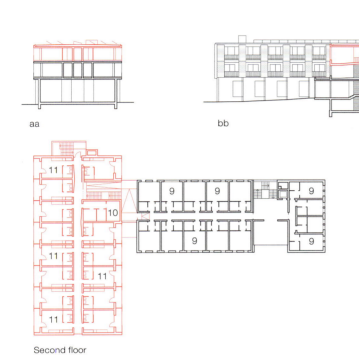

aa   bb

Second floor

First floor

b

Ground floor

sps architekten

Site plan
Scale 1:2500
Sections · floor plans
Scale 1:750

1   Secondary entrance
2   Foyer
3   Hall
4   Lounge / lobby
5   Seminar rooms
6   Bar
7   Kitchen
8   Restaurant
9   Double room (existing)
10 Cleaner / storeroom
11 Double room (new build)

Andrew Phelps

Andrew Phelps

Vertical section · horizontal section
Scale 1:20

1 Parapet coping, galvanized
 30 mm larch three-layer
 30 mm framing / rear ventilation
 100 mm timber construction / mineral wool
 thermal insulation
 80 mm timber construction / mineral wool
 thermal insulation
 20 mm plywood panel, vapour barrier
2 60/8 mm flat steel hollow section frame for
 60/30 mm larch timber slats, painted
3 100 mm extensive green roof
 geotextile fleece, 25 mm drainage mat
 two-layer bituminous waterproofing, root-resistant
 average 140 mm insulation to falls

160 mm mineral wool thermal insulation
vapour barrier, 140 mm cross-laminated timber
4 30 mm larch sheathing
 30 mm framing / rear ventilation, windtight layer, 2× 120 mm timber construction /
 mineral wool thermal insulation, vapour barrier
 80 mm cross-laminated timber
5 25 mm larch floorboards
 60/60 mm battens on height-adjustable
 pedestals
 waterproofing
 80 mm cross-laminated timber (installed to falls)
 300/200 mm spruce beams
 22 mm larch three layer panel
6 150/200 mm steel angle rigid support
7 140/200 mm timber support
 elastomeric bearing

8 25 mm parquet
 2× 12.5 mm gypsum fibreboard
 30 mm impact soundproofing
 50 mm levelling fill, PE foil
 120 mm cross-laminated timber
 140 mm mineral wool, waterproofing
 200 mm reinforced concrete slab (existing)
9 2× 12.5 mm gypsum board
 50 mm metal studs, mineral wool insulation fill,
 5 mm air cavity
 80 mm cross-laminated timber
10 80 mm cross-laminated timber
 2× 12.5 mm gypsum board
 2× 30 mm mineral wool wall cavity insulation
 2× 12.5 mm gypsum board
 80 mm cross-laminated timber
11 30 mm partition wall, larch three layer panel,
 painted

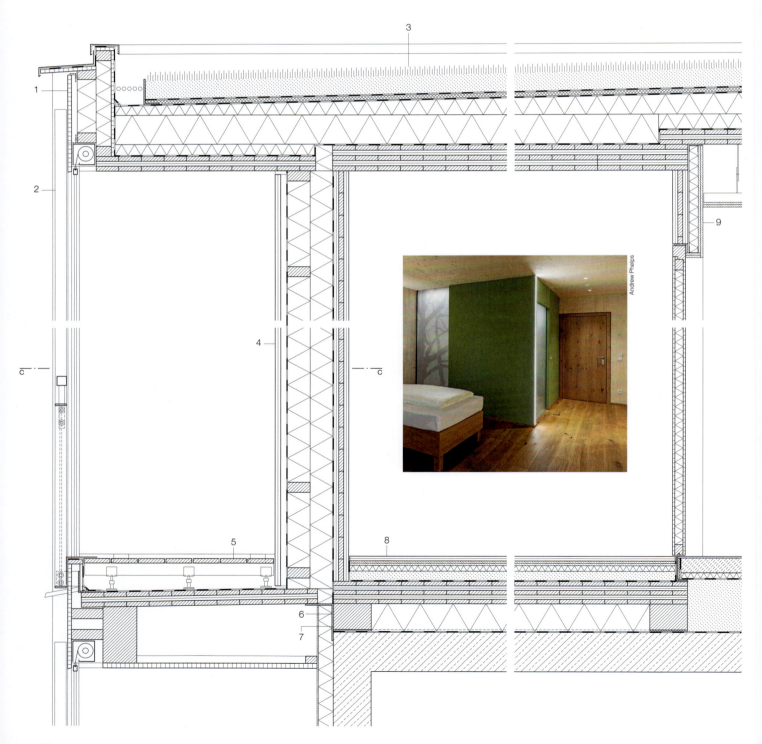

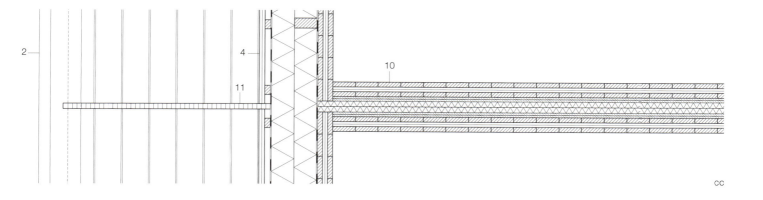

Andrew Phelps

Town House in Vevey

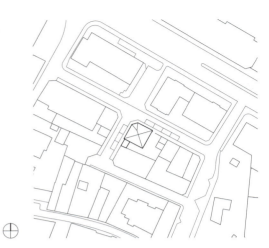

Architecture: Rapin Saiz Architectes,
                               Vevey (CH)
Structural engineering: Ratio Bois Sàrl, Cuarny (CH)
Building services: Sacao, Fribourg (CH)

The 19th-century residence is situated in a former artisanal quarter of Vevey on Lake Geneva. It is one of the historical buildings recognized as being of cultural value in the town, and the renovation was to retain the character of the edifice. With only a few carefully conceived interventions, Rapin Saiz Architekten successfully transformed the listed residence, while defining a new, highly recognisable identity for the building within the neighbourhood.

The existing volume, a three-storey solid-walled masonry structure with external access balconies in timber, which had been altered and extended continually in the past, was badly in need of refurbishment in addition to lacking modern sanitary facilities. In the course of the alterations, not only were all three flats completely refurbished but also the external access balconies now serve as a winter garden for each flat. The building also gained a new roof storey, which stands out in terms of construction and colour from the existing fabric. The topmost flat features a generous living space that receives ample daylight. The walls painted white conceal prefabricated floor-to-floor height timber frame elements. They received an interior layer of gypsum board and insulation on site. Due to structural concerns, a timber concrete composite slab was set on top of the existing structure. The actual addition consists of timber, due to its low weight and short, prefabrication-based construction time. The elegant interplay of the existing building and the vertical extension is most of all obvious on the south-eastern side: the new parts of the building are oriented towards the existing winter gardens and emphasize their rhythmic structure. The ox-blood red paint unifies the old and the new.

Site plan
Scale 1:2000
Floor plans · section
Scale 1:250

1   Entrance
2   Corridor
3   Cooking/eating
4   Veranda
5   Apartment
6   Bedroom
7   Studio
8   Office
9   Living/eating

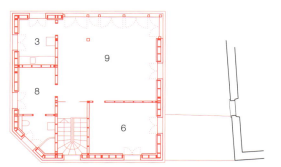

Rooftop floor

aa

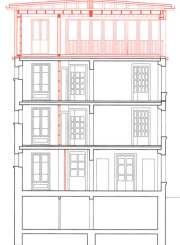

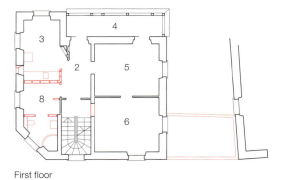

First floor

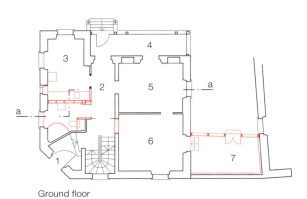

Ground floor

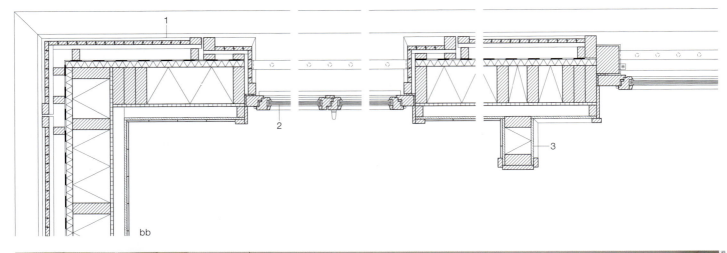

bb

Horizontal section · vertical section
Scale 1:20

1 60 mm timber panel, solid larch, painted
   40/60 mm counter battens, wind barrier
   35 mm wood fibre thermal insulation
   60/200 mm timber stud framing, 200 mm mineral
   wool thermal insulation fill
   vapour barrier, 15 mm OSB board
   40/60 mm battens / services cavity
   12.5 mm gypsum fibreboard, butt joints concealed
   with timber battens
2 Window: double glazing in wood frame
3 12.5 mm gypsum fibreboard
   60/140 mm timber stud framing, 140 mm mineral
   wool thermal insulation fill
   12.5 mm gypsum fibreboard
4 2 mm standing seam roofing
   breathable underlay; 27 mm wood-based panel
   60 mm battens / rear ventilation
   waterproofing membrane,
   27 mm three layer panel

120 mm softwood rafters
5 Box ceiling: 60 mm wood fibreboard
   60/200 mm ceiling beams
   200 mm mineral wool thermal insulation fill
   vapour barrier, 27 mm spruce three layer panel
   80/180 mm rafters
6 60 mm timber panel, solid larch, painted
   40/60 mm counter battens
   wind paper, 35 mm wood fibre thermal insulation
   40 mm wood fibre thermal insulation
   160 mm glued laminated timber
   80 mm services cavity
   27 mm spruce three layer panel
7 14 mm oak parquet
   70 mm screed
   40 mm impact soundproofing
   Timber-concrete composite ceiling:
   80 mm reinforced concrete, separating layer
   35 mm 3-ply cross laminated timber
   180 mm timber beam ceiling (existing)
   35 mm 3-ply cross-laminated timber
8 500 mm masonry (existing)

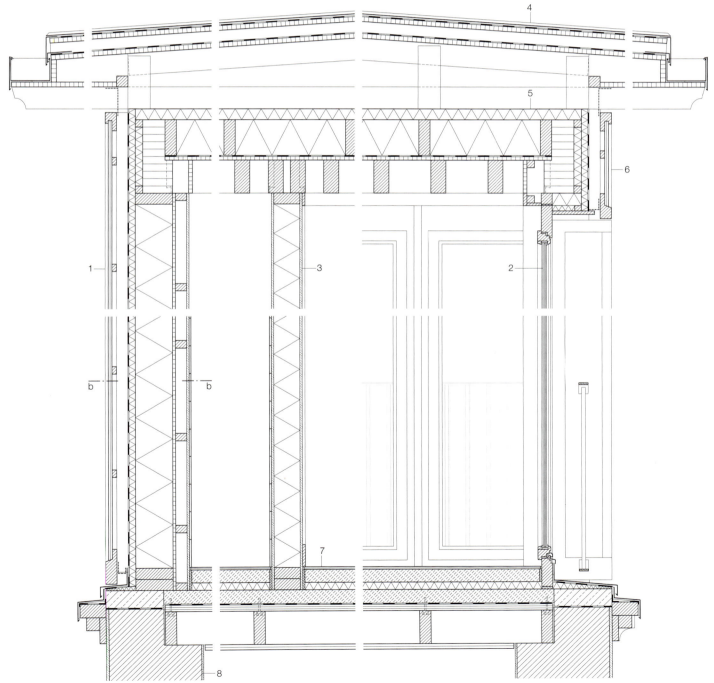

Library in London

Architecture:	studio weave, London (GB)
Client:	London Borough of Waltham Forest, London (GB)
Structural engineering:	Andrew Trotman, Timber-wright, Berkhamsted (GB)
Landscape architecture:	Tom Massey Studio, London (GB)
Interior architecture:	Sebastian Cox, London (GB)

The extension to the Lea Bridge Library in the London Borough of Waltham Forest enriches the existing library, a listed red-brick building from 1905, and extends across the whole western side of the plot along an adjacent firewall.

Entry is provided by a new barrier-free access, which also serves as a social hub for the whole district. In addition to a café, the addition houses informal reading areas for library users and extensive bookshelves with integrated niches and seats along the back wall. Room-height glazing along the whole length of the building offers unobstructed views on to the adjoining Friendship Garden and creates a connection to the surrounding greenery. The wood species selected for the interiors include poplar, ash, oak, sequoia and horse chestnut, used for the wall surfaces and integrated furniture. A semi-circular recess in the center of the facade protects the roots of a mature lime tree. Here, the indoor space is subdivided by a large circular sliding door to accommodate this feature.

The load-bearing structure of the extension is fabricated from laminated veneer lumber and spans between the brick wall of the existing building and a colonnade of red precast concrete elements. The timber beams, however, do not rest on the old masonry but rather on columns integrated into a new thermally insulated timber construction standing at a distance of 10 cm in front of the existing wall.

On the garden side, the roof construction is supported by steel columns clad with precast concrete elements. The colonnade protects the timber construction from severe weather and its columns conceal the downpipes serving to drain water from the roof, which is used to irrigate the trees.

Jim Stephenson

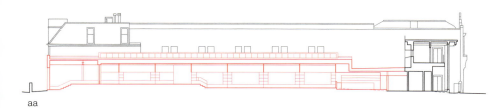

aa

bb

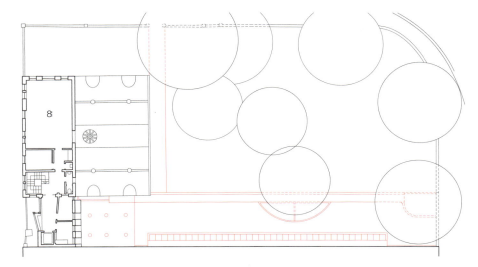

First floor

Site plan
Scale 1:5000
Sections · floor plans
Scale 1:500

1   Main entrance
2   Secondary entrance, existing building
3   Computer desks
4   Library
5   Cafeteria
6   Work desks
7   Light well
8   Meeting room

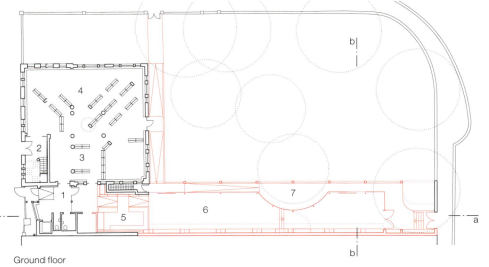

Ground floor

Vertical section
Scale 1:20

1 Masonry, rendered (existing)
2 2 mm steel sheet flashing
3 3 mm canted sheet aluminium
  10 mm sheathing
  thermal insulation to falls
  single bituminous waterproofing layer
  12 mm OSB
  200/50 mm wood blocking, 2× 90 mm PUR
  rigid foam insulation fill
  vapour barrier
  18 mm OSB
4 Skylight: double glazing in aluminium frame
5 Galvanized corrugated sheet steel, self-drilling
  screw connections, incl. sealing washer
  50/70 mm battens
  50/70 mm counter battens
  synthetic waterproofing membrane
  12 mm OSB
  180/40 mm timber rafters, 2× 90 mm rigid
  foam insulation fill in between
  vapour barrier
  18 mm OSB
  suspended ceiling:
  acoustic ceiling element consisting of
  30 mm mineral wool insulation
  18 mm wood fibreboard
  2.5 mm black acoustic fleece
  10 mm oak slats, placed at intervals
6 UPN 200 steel channel
7 Sliding window: double glazing in aluminium
  frame
8 2 mm stainless steel rainwater channel
  roof waterproofing membrane overlapped and
  welded
  12 mm OSB board
  160–130 mm laminated veneer lumber beam
  to falls
  45/55 mm counter battens
  25 mm oak sheathing
9 230 mm steel channel
10 20 mm precast reinforced concrete cladding
11 80/80 mm steel SHS column
12 20 mm oak panelling, offset from wall
   18 mm MDF board framing
   services cavity
   12 mm plywood panelling
   25/25 mm battens, vapour barrier
   12 mm OSB
   195/45 mm timber studs, 2× 90 mm rigid
   foam insulation fill
   12 mm OSB
   separating layer
   rear ventilation
   rendered masonry (existing)
13 25 mm back wall panel, various wood species,
   e.g. horse chestnut
14 12 mm back wall seat, various wood species,
   e.g. ash
15 70 mm polished screed
   separating layer
   120 mm rigid foam insulation
   vapour barrier
   250 mm reinforced concrete

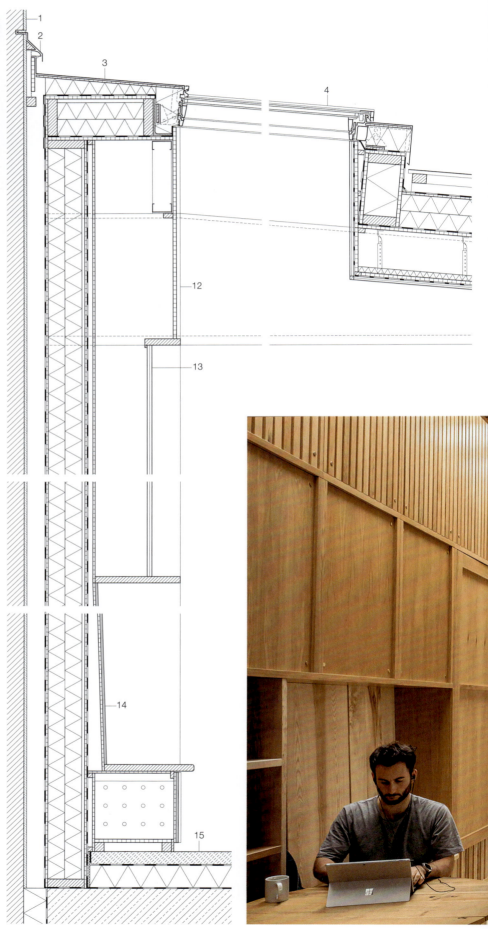

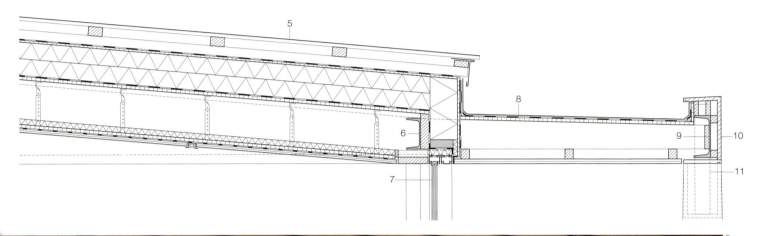

Commercial Building in Thalgau

Architecture: dunkelschwarz, Salzburg (AT)
Client: PCT Austria, Thalgau (AT)
Building physics: Ingenieurbüro Rothbacher,
                     Zell am See (AT)
Lighting: Licht Art, Thalgau (AT)

Viewed from the exterior, the hall displays a special character, situated in the middle of a dispersed and heterogeneous industrial zone in the Austrian town of Thalgau. The carefully designed open space indicates that this is not a purely functional building but instead a headquarters truly representative of the company, where customers and staff alike are intended to feel comfortable.

The double folding gate, clad in wood siding in bright hues, reveals the impression of an inserted timber box. Both contrast strongly with the otherwise dark facade. The existing building, a very simple reinforced concrete structure, remains largely untouched. Only the undersides of the roof were refurbished, the facades painted black and an additional opening created in the side wall.

Access to the interior of the 21.50 × 7.25 m timber box is provided by a retractable metal platform. Up to 14 workplaces are available on a total floor area of 250 m², split between two levels. On the ground floor, a precast concrete table offers a central meeting point for customers and staff. The staff offices are located in the back of the space. The meeting room and managers' rooms are on the upper floor. The compact "building within a building" shares the main elements of the existing fabric such as roof, facade and services infrastructure. However, in contrast to the warehouse, its heating is provided by a heat pump. The box serves as a thermal envelope and consists of solid spruce cross-laminated timber. The butt joints between elements display visibly exposed screw connections. The 28 cm thick solid timber walls create a pleasant indoor climate and require no further thermal insulation. This minimalist structure saves costs not only during construction but also during operation.

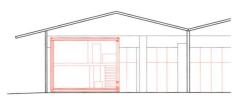

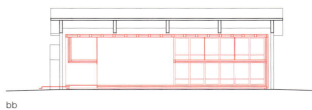

aa   bb

Site plan
Scale 1:10 000
Sections · floor plans
Scale 1:400

1   Entrance
2   Reception/
    communication/
    staff area
3   Office
4   Archive
5   Warehouse with
    high-rack shelving
6   Covered seating area/
    pergola
7   Heated store
8   Neighbouring building
    (existing)
9   Utilities/storeroom
10 Air space
11 Meeting room

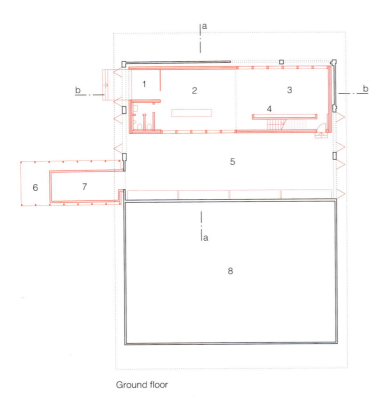

Ground floor

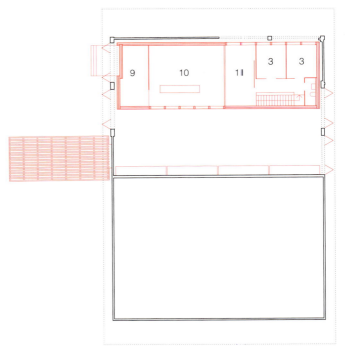

Upper floor

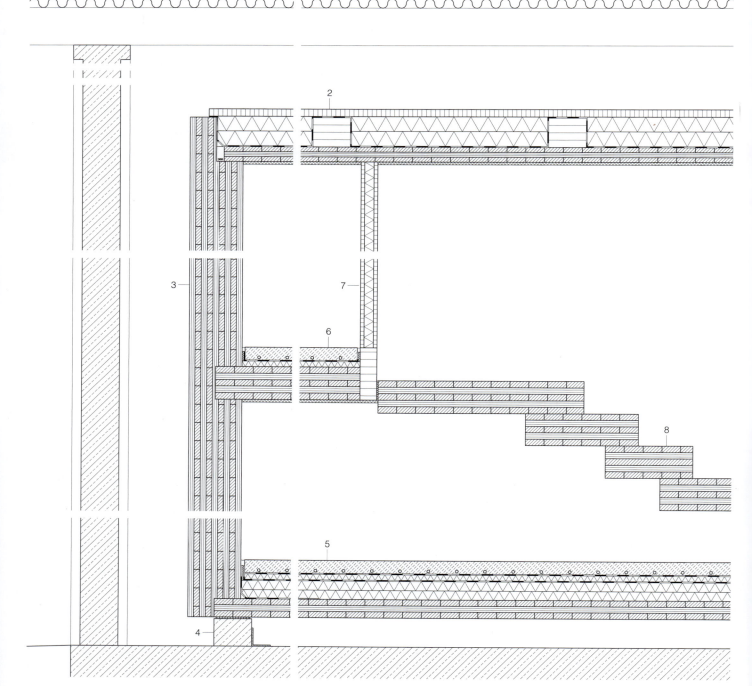

Vertical section
Scale 1:20

1 Roof (existing)
2 Roof construction of box:
    40 mm wood-based roofing, walkable
    200/160 mm glued laminated timber beam
    2× 80 mm wood fibre insulation board fill
    bituminous vapour barrier with aluminium inlay
    80 mm cross-laminated timber
    15 mm wood wool acoustic panel
3 Wall construction:
    280 mm cross-laminated timber panel,
    black glazed finish
4 Concrete strip foundation with
    PUR elastomeric bearing
    secured by steel angle
5 Ground floor construction:
    70 mm trowel-finished heating screed

PE foil
30 mm impact soundproofing
sealant foil
2× 50 mm wood fibre insulation
100 mm cross-laminated timber panel
6 Upper floor construction:
    70 mm trowel-finished heating screed
    PE foil
    30 mm impact soundproofing
    180 mm cross-laminated timber
    15 mm wood wool acoustic panel
7 Wall construction:
    19 mm three layer panel
    C-section metal studs, wood wool fill
    19 mm three layer panel
8 175 mm solid cross-laminated timber treads,
    planed
9 19 mm three layer panel fall protection
10 Triple glazing in wood frame

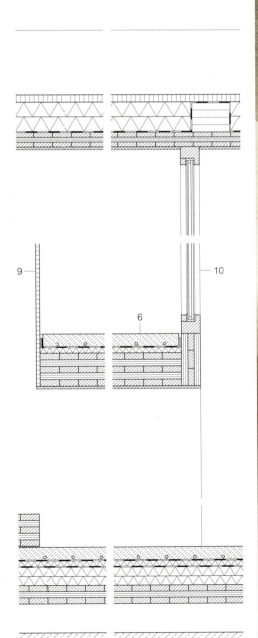

Simon Oberhofer

Authors

Stefan Krötsch
Prof. Dipl.-Ing. Architekt BDA
1994–2001 Studied architecture at the Technical University of Munich (TUM) and the Wroclaw University of Science and Technology in Wroclaw, Poland
2001–2003 Worked at bogevischs büro, Munich
2003–2005 Project Manager at Söldner und Stender Architekten, Munich
2005–2013 Stefan Krötsch Architectural Practice in Munich
2008–2014 Scientific Assistant at the Chair of Timber Construction Prof. Hermann Kaufmann, Technical University of Munich
2009–2019 Braun Krötsch Architekten in partnership with Florian Braun
2015–2018 Assistant Professor, Head of the newly established Chair of Tectonics in Timber Construction, Department of Architecture at the Technical University of Kaiserslautern
2018– Professor of Building Construction and Design at the HTWG Konstanz – University of Applied Sciences
2020 Appointment to the Association of German Architects (BDA) Bavaria, member of the board and expert adviser on climate-compatible building
2020– Klingelhöfer Krötsch Architekten in partnership with Ruth Klingelhöfer-Krötsch

Manfred Stieglmeier
Prof. M.Eng. Dipl.-Ing. (FH) Architekt
Studied architecture at the Academy of Fine Arts Munich and at the Munich University of Applied Sciences
1987–1998 Worked at various architectural offices in Munich including Auer + Weber
1999–2000 Partner at Schmidhuber + Partner
2000– Freelance architect, with own architectural practice Stieglmeier Architekten in Munich specializing in timber construction
2007–2009 Master's Degree in Timber Construction for Architects at the Rosenheim University of Applied Sciences
2009–2021 Scientific Assistant to the Professor of Architectural Design and Timber Construction Prof. Hermann Kaufmann, Technical University of Munich
2017– Member of the Charta für Holz 2.0 Working Group of the German Federal Ministry of Food and Agriculture (BMEL)
2019–2020 Lectureship at the Salzburg University of Applied Sciences (FH Salzburg), course title: Forest Products Technology & Timber Constructions
2021– Professor at the Salzburg University of Applied Sciences, program title: Green Building – Design & Engineering, specializing in Building Design

Thomas Engel
Dr.-Ing. Civil Engineer
2006–2013 Studied civil engineering at the Technical University of Munich
2014–2017 Project Manager for fire protection design and fire engineering at hhpberlin Ingenieure für den Brandschutz GmbH
2015– Chief of a division of the Munich Volunteer Fire Brigade
2017–2021 Fire protection engineer and specialist for the fire safety consultancy FIRE & TIMBER .ING
2017– Research Associate at the Chair of Timber Structures and Building Construction at the Technical University of Munich and Project Manager of the federal research projects TIMpuls and Fire-SafeGreen
2022– Managing Director and founder of Brandschutz-Engel GmbH and KET Fire GmbH
2023 Doctorate at the Technical University of Munich: "Fire Engineering for Sustainable Facades – Experimental Investigations for Fire-Safe Facade Design"
2023– Group Lead Fire Research at the Chair of Timber Structures and Building Construction at the Technical University of Munich

Thomas Stark
Prof. Dr.-Ing. Architekt
Trained as qualified bank clerk
Studied architecture and awarded doctorate at the University of Stuttgart
2003–2005 Scientific Assistant at the Chair of Building Construction 2, Prof. Stefan Behling, University of Stuttgart
2005–2008 Scientific Assistant in the Department of Design and Energy-Efficient Building under Professor Manfred Hegger at the Technical University of Darmstadt
2003 Founded ee-plan, Stuttgart
2008– Professor of Energy-Efficient Building at the HTWG Konstanz – University of Applied Sciences, Faculty of Architecture and Design
2009– Managing Partner of ee concept GmbH, Darmstadt/Tübingen

Annette Hafner
Prof. Dr.-Ing. Architektin
1990–1997 Studied architecture at the Technical University of Munich and the Barcelona School of Architecture (ETSAB)
1998–2004 Architect in London and Munich
2004–2014 Scientific Assistant at the Chair of Timber Structures and Building Construction Prof. Winter and Head of the ZQ MPA BAU certification body at the Technical University of Munich
2012 Doctorate at the Faculty of Civil Engineering and Land Surveying, Technical University of Munich
2014– Professor at the Chair of Resource-Efficient Building at the Ruhr University Bochum, Faculty of Civil and Environmental Engineering

Photos introducing topics
Page 4: Conversion of a residential and commercial building into student flats, Ernas Haus, Dornbirn (AT) 2020, Ludescher + Lutz Architekten
Photo: E. Ludescher
Page 6: Connection of the new timber floor to the existing floor, additional storeys and extension in timber construction, Deutscher Alpenverein (DAV) Headquarters, Munich (DE) 2021, ELEMENT A. Architekten, hiendl_schineis architektenpartnerschaft
Photo: ELEMENT A. Architekten
Page 24: Delivery of a prefabricated timber panel construction element for the modernization of a residential and commercial building, Munich (DE) 2016, Braun Krötsch Architekten
Photo: Florian Braun
Page 48: Two-storey roof extension, timber hybrid construction, housing complex, Salzburg (AT) 2021, cs-architektur
Photo: Volker Wortmeyer
Page 72: Two-and-a-half-storey roof extension with a gable roof and dormers, town house in Linz (AT) 2020, mia2 Architektur
Photo: Kurt Hörbst

Subject Index

A Selection of Available Titles

DETAIL Practice

Green Facades
2024
Nicole Pfoser
120 pages, format 21 × 29.7 cm

Hardcover:
EUR 54.90 / GBP 44.– / USD 74.–
ISBN: 978-3-95553-620-6

E-Book:
EUR 54.90 / GBP 44.– / USD 74.–
ISBN: 978-3-95553-621-3

Hybrid Construction
2022
Oliver Fischer, Werner Lang,
Stefan Winter
96 pages, format 21 × 29.7 cm

Hardcover:
EUR 52.90 / GBP 42.– / USD 71.–
ISBN: 978-3-95553-575-9

E-Book:
EUR 52.90 / GBP 42.– / USD 71.–
ISBN: 978-3-95553-576-6

Building with Hardwood
2021
Konrad Merz, Anne Niemann,
Stefan Torno
112 pages, format 21 × 29.7 cm

Hardcover:
EUR 52.90 / GBP 42.– / USD 71.–
ISBN 978-3-95553-559-9

E-Book:
EUR 52.90 / GBP 42.– / USD 71.–
ISBN 978-3-95553-560-5

Building in Timber – Room Modules
2019
Wolfgang Huss, Matthias
Kaufmann, Konrad Merz
112 pages, format 21 × 29.7 cm

Hardcover:
EUR 52.90 / GBP 42.– / USD 71.–
ISBN 978-3-95553-494-3

E-Book:
EUR 52.90 / GBP 42.– / USD 71.–
ISBN 978-3-95553-495-0

Stairs
2018
Christian Peter, Christine Peter,
Daniel Reisch, Katinka Temme
120 pages, format 21 × 29.7 cm

Hardcover:
EUR 52.90 / GBP 42.– / USD 71.–
ISBN 978-3-95553-397-7

E-Book:
EUR 52.90 / GBP 42.– / USD 71.–
ISBN 978-3-95553-398-4

Flooring Volume 1
2016
José Luis Moro
120 pages, format 21 × 29.7 cm

Paperback:
EUR 39.90 / GBP 32.– / USD 53.–
ISBN 978-3-95553-301-4

E-Book:
EUR 39.90 / GBP 32.– / USD 53.–
ISBN 978-3-95553-302-1

Flooring Volume 2
2016
José Luis Moro
120 pages, format 21 × 29.7 cm

Paperback:
EUR 39.90 / GBP 32.– / USD 53.–
ISBN 978-3-95553-313-7

E-Book:
EUR 39.90 / GBP 32.– / USD 53.–
ISBN 978-3-95553-314-4

Bathrooms and Sanitation
2015
Sibylle Kramer
120 pages, format 21 × 29.7 cm

Paperback:
EUR 39.90 / GBP 32.– / USD 53.–
ISBN 978-3-95553-232-1

E-Book:
EUR 39.90 / GBP 32.– / USD 53.–
ISBN 978-3-95553-233-8

Colour
2014
Axel Buether
120 pages, format 21 × 29.7 cm

Paperback:
EUR 52.90 / GBP 42.– / USD 74.–
ISBN 978-3-95553-208-6

E-Book:
EUR 52.90 / GBP 42.– / USD 74.–
ISBN 978-3-95553-209-3

Pedestrian Bridges
2013
Andreas Keil
112 pages, format 21 × 29.7 cm

Paperback:
EUR 39.90 / GBP 32.– / USD 55.–
ISBN 978-3-920034-91-1

E-Book:
EUR 39.90 / GBP 32.– / USD 55.–
ISBN 978-3-95553-147-8

Photovoltaics
2010
Bernhard Weller and others
112 pages, format 21 × 29.7 cm

Paperback:
EUR 42.95 / GBP 35.– / USD 60.–
ISBN 978-3-0346-0369-0

E-Book:
EUR 42.95 / GBP 35.– / USD 60.–
ISBN 978-3-0346-1570-9

Barrier-Free Design
2010
Oliver Heiss, Johann Ebe,
Christine Degenhart
112 pages, format 21 × 29.7 cm

Paperback:
EUR 42.95 / GBP 35.– / USD 60.–
ISBN 978-3-0346-0577-9

E-Book:
EUR 42.95 / GBP 35.– / USD 60.–
ISBN 978-3-0346-1572-3